Great Essays | **4**

GREAT WRITING

FIFTH EDITION
Keith S. Folse
April Muchmore-Vokoun
Elena Vestri

NATIONAL GEOGRAPHIC
LEARNING

Australia · Brazil · Mexico · Singapore · United Kingdom · United States

Great Writing 4: Great Essays
Keith S. Folse, April Muchmore-Vokoun,
Elena Vestri

Publisher: Sherrise Roehr

Executive Editor: Laura Le Dréan

Managing Editor: Jennifer Monaghan

Director of Global Marketing: Ian Martin

Product Marketing Manager: Tracy Bailie

Senior Director, Production: Michael Burggren

Production Manager: Daisy Sosa

Content Project Manager: Mark Rzeszutek

Manufacturing Planner: Mary Beth Hennebury

Art Director: Brenda Carmichael

Interior Design: Lisa Trager

Cover Design: Lisa Trager

Composition: SPi-Global

For permission to use material from this text or product,
submit all requests online at **www.cengage.com/permissions**
Further permissions questions can be emailed to
permissionrequest@cengage.com

Student Edition: 978-0-357-02085-2
Student Edition with Online Workbook Access Code: 978-0-357-02108-8

National Geographic Learning
20 Channel Center Street
Boston, MA 02210
USA

Cengage learning is a leading provider of customized learning solutions with office locations around the globe, including Singapore, the United Kingdom, Australia, Mexico, Brazil, and Japan. Locate our local office at: **International. cengage.com/region**

Cengage Learning products are represented in Canada by Nelson Education, Ltd.

Visit NGL online at **ELTNGL.com**

Visit our corporate website at **cengage.com**

Printed in China
Print Number: 01   Print Year: 2019

CREDITS

Cover © Yimei Sun/Moment/Getty Images

Unit 01 Page 2-3: © Mikayla A Wujec/National Geographic Creative; Page 4: © Arterra Picture Library/Alamy Stock Photo; Page 6: © Martchan/Shutterstock.com; Page 8: © mehmettorlak/E+/Getty Images; Page 10: © Goran Bogicevic/Shutterstock.com; Page 12: © SIHASAKPRACHUM/Shutterstock.com; Page 12: © KatKrittimook/Shutterstock.com; Page 15: © Hero Images/Getty Images; Page 22: © Ron Galella/Ron Galella Collection/Getty Images; Page 25: © KidStock/Blend Images/Getty Images; Page 25: © Monkey Business Images/Shutterstock.com; Page 14: © William Yu Photography/Moment Open/Getty Images; Page 29: © Hero Images/Getty Images

Unit 02 Page 38-39: © Mangiwau/Moment/Getty Images; Page 41: © Andrew Hasson/Alamy Stock Photo; Page 47: © wavebreakmedia/Shutterstock.com; Page 49: © Felix Vogel/imageBROKER/Getty Images; Page 52: © Blend Images - Jeremy Woodhouse/Brand X Pictures/Getty Images; Page 57: © Tom Dulat/Getty Images Entertainment/Getty Images; Page 61: © Corey Rich/Aurora Photos; Page 51: © JULIE MAYFENG/National Geographic Creative; Page 44: © John Duncan/EyeEm/Getty Images; Page 65: © FilippoBacci/E+/Getty Images

Unit 03 Page 68-69: © David Guttenfelder/National Geographic Creative; Page 70: © Walter Bibikow/Photolibrary/Getty Images; Page 72: © TASSO MARCELO/AFP/Getty Images; Page 72: © wundervisuals/E+/Getty Images; Page 77: © Elli Thor Magnusson/Cultura/Getty Images; Page 80: © seanscott/RooM/Getty Images; Page 86: © Richard Paul Kane/Shutterstock.com; Page 86: © Gualter Fatia/Getty Images Sport/Getty Images; Page 85: © Whitepointer/Deposit Photos; Page 74: © Anna Gibiskys/Moment/Getty Images; Page 91: © Doug Gimesy; Page 94: © Kohei Hara/DigitalVision/Getty Images

Unit 04 Page 96-97: © JOEL SARTORE/National Geographic Creative; Page 99: © Klaus Vedfelt/DigitalVision/Getty Images; Page 104: © Thomas Trutschel/Photothek/Getty Images; Page 106: © National Geographic Creative/Alamy Stock Photo; Page 109: © Gallo Images/Shutterstock.com; Page 120: © ton koene/Alamy Stock Photo; Page 110: © Michael Fitzsimmons/Shutterstock.com

Unit 05 Page 124-125: © LYNN JOHNSON/National Geographic Creative; Page 129: © ffoto_travel/Alamy Stock Photo; Page 131: © ROMEO GACAD/AFP/Getty Images; Page 136-137: © Westend61/Getty Images; Page 135: © Mark Stone/National Geographic Creative; Page 141: © St. Louis Post-Dispatch/Tribune News Service/Getty Images

Unit 06 Page 148-149: © Matt Moyer; Page 152: © Bob Daemmrich/Alamy Stock Photo; Page 154: © World History Archive/Alamy Stock Photo; Page 156: © Quang nguyen vinh/Shutterstock.com; Page 169: © VINCENT JANNINK/AFP/Getty Images; Page 163: © Dan Kitwood/Getty Images News/Getty Images; Page 167: © Clement McCarthy/Alamy Stock Photo;

Text Credits: Page 169: Caryl-Sue, National Geographic, February 21, 2013. https://www.nationalgeographic.org/media/strange-rains-wbt/

CONTENTS

GREAT WRITING MAKES GREAT WRITERS

The new edition of *Great Writing* provides clear explanations, academic writing models, and focused practice to help students write great sentences, paragraphs, and essays. Every unit has expanded vocabulary building, sentence development, and more structured final writing tasks.

National Geographic images and content spark students' imaginations and inspire their writing.

Each unit includes:

PART 1: Elements of Great Writing teaches the fundamentals of writing.

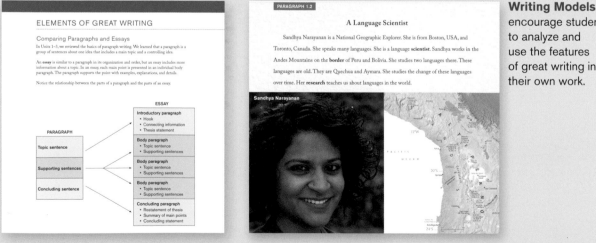

Writing Models encourage students to analyze and use the features of great writing in their own work.

Targeted Grammar presents clear explanations and examples that students can immediately apply to their work.

PART 2: Building Better Vocabulary highlights academic words, word associations, collocations, word forms, and vocabulary for writing.

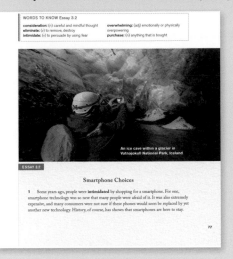

New Words to Know boxes throughout each unit target carefully-leveled words students will frequently use.

PART 3: Building Better Sentences focuses students on sentence-level work to ensure more accurate writing.

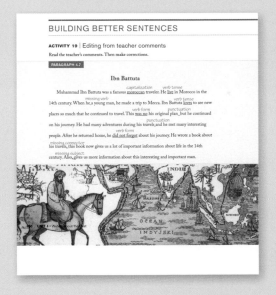

PART 4: Writing activities allow students to apply what they have learned by guiding them through the process of writing, editing, and revising.

NEW Test Prep section prepares students for timed writing on high-stakes tests.

SUPPORT FOR INSTRUCTORS AND STUDENTS

FOR INSTRUCTORS

The Classroom Presentation Tool brings the classroom to life by including all Student Book pages, answers, and games to practice vocabulary.

Assessment: ExamView allows instructors to create custom tests and quizzes in minutes. **ExamView** and **Ready to Go Tests** are available online at the teacher companion website for ease of use.

FOR STUDENTS

The Online Workbook provides additional practice in vocabulary, grammar, and writing, plus remediation activities for students who have not mastered at-level vocabulary and grammar.

NEW Guided online writing practice reinforces the writing process, helping students become stronger and more independent writers.

ACKNOWLEDGEMENTS

The Authors and Publisher would like to acknowledge and thank the teachers around the world who participated in the development of the fifth edition of *Great Writing*.

Asia

Anthony Brian Gallagher, Meijo University, Nagoya

Atsuko Aoki, Aoyama Gakuin University, Tokyo

Atsushi Taguchi, Okayama University of Science, Imabari Campus, Ehime

Helen Hanae, Reitaku University, Kashiwa

Hiroko Shikano, Juchi Medical University, Gotemba

Hisashi Shigematsu, Toyo Gakeun University, Tokyo

Jeremiah L. Hall, Meijo University, Nagoya

Jian Liang Fu, Kwansei Gakuin University, Nishinomiya

Jim Hwang, Yonsei University, Asan

John C. Pulaski, Chuo University and Tokyo Woman's Christian University, Tokyo

Junyawan Suwannarat, Chiang Mai University, Chiang Mai

Katherine Bauer, Clark Memorial International High School, Chiba

Kazuyo Ishibashi, Aoyama Gakuin Univeristy, Tokyo

Lei Na, Jump A-Z, Nanjing

Lor Kiat Seng, Southern University College, Seremban

Mark McClure, Kansai Gaidai Univeristy, Osaka

Matthew Shapiro, Konan Boys High School, Ashiya

Nattalak Thirachotikun, Chiang Mai University, Chiang Rai

Nick Boyes, Meijo University, Nagoya

Nick Collier, Ritsumeikan Uji Junior and Senior High School, Kobe

Olesya Shatunova, Kanagawa University, Yokohama

Pattanapichet Fasawang, Bangkok University International College, Bangkok

Paul Hansen, Hokkaido University, Sapporo

Paul Salisbury, Aichi University, Nagoya

Randall Cotten, Gifu City Women's College, Gifu

Sayaka Karlin, Toyo Gakuen University, Tokyo

Scott Gray, Clark Memorial International High School Umeda Campus, Osaka

Selina Richards, HELP University, Kuala Lumpur

Terrelle Bernard Griffin, No. 2 High School of East China Normal University-International Division, Shanghai

William Pellowe, Kinki University, Fukuoka

Yoko Hirase, Hiroshima Kokusai Gakuin University, Hiroshima

Youngmi Lim, Shinshu University, Matsumoto

Zachary Fish, RDFZ Xishan School AP Center, Beijing

USA

Amanda Kmetz, BIR Training Center, Chicago, Illinois

Amy Friedman, The American Language Institute, San Diego, California

Amy Litman, College of Southern Nevada, Las Vegas, Nevada

Angela Lehman, Virginia Commonwealth University, Richmond, Virginia

Aylin Bunk, Mount Hood Community College, Portland, Oregon

Barbara Silas, South Seattle College, Seattle, Washington

Bette Brickman, College of Southern Nevada, Las Vegas, Nevada

Breana Bayraktar, Northern Virginia Community College, Fairfax, Virginia

Carolyn Ho, Lone Star College-CyFair, Cypress, Texas

Celeste Flowers, University of Central Arkansas, Conway, Arkansas

Christina Abella, The College of Chicago, Chicago, Illinois

Christine Lines, College of Southern Nevada, Las Vegas, Nevada

Clare Roh, Howard Community College, Columbia, Maryland

DeLynn MacQueen, Columbus State Community College, Columbus, Ohio

Eleanor Molina, Northern Essex Community College, Lawrence, Massachusetts

Emily Brown, Hillsborough Community College, Florida

Emily Cakounes, North Shore Community College, Medford, Massachusetts

Erica Lederman, BIR Training Center, Chicago, Illinois

Erin Zoranski, Delaware Technical Community College, Wilmington, Delaware

Eugene Polissky, University of Potomac, Washington, DC

Farideh Hezaveh, Northern Virginia Community College, Sterling, Virginia

Gretchen Hack, Community College of Denver, Denver, Colorado

Heather Snavely, California Baptist University, Riverside, California

Hilda Tamen, University of Texas Rio Grande Valley, Edinburg, Texas

Holly Milkowart, Johnson County Community College, Overland Park, Kansas

Jessica Weimer, Cascadia College, Bothell, Washington

Jill Pagels, Lonestar Community College, Houston, Texas

Jonathan Murphy, Virginia Commonwealth University, Richmond, Virginia

Joseph Starr, Houston Community College, Southwest, Houston, Texas

Judy Chmielecki, Northern Essex Community College, Lawrence, Massachusetts

Kate Baldridge-Hale, Valencia College, Orlando, Florida

Kathleen Biache, Miami Dade College, Miami, Florida

Katie Edwards, Howard Community College, Columbia, Maryland

Kenneth Umland, College of Southern Nevada, Las Vegas, Nevada

Kevin Bowles, Linfield College, McMinnville, Oregon
Kim Hardiman, University of Central Florida, Orlando, Florida
Kori Zunic, San Diego City College, San Diego, California
Kris Lowrey, Virginia Commonwealth University, Richmond, Virginia
Kristin Homuth, Language Center International, Oak Park, Michigan
Leon Palombo, Miami Dade College, North Campus, Miami Beach, Florida
Lily Jaffie-Shupe, Virginia Polytechnic Institute, Blacksburg, Virginia
Lisse Hildebrandt, Virginia Commonwealth University, Richmond, Virginia
Luba Nesterova, Bilingual Education Institute, Houston, Texas
Madhulika Tandon, Lone Star College, University Park, Houston, Texas

Matthew Wolpert, Virginia Commonwealth University, Richmond, Virginia
Megan Nestor, Seattle Central College, Seattle, Washington
Meredith Kemper, University of Central Arkansas, Conway, Arkansas
Mike Sfiropoulos, Palm Beach State College, Lake Worth, Florida
Milena Eneva, Chattahoochee Technical College, Atlanta, Georgia
Myra M. Medina, Miami Dade College, Miami, Florida
Naomi Klimowicz, Howard Community College, Columbia, Maryland
Nicholas C. Zefran, Northern Virginia Community College, Springfield, Virginia
Nicole Ianieri, East Carolina University, Greenville, North Carolina
Patricia Nation, Miami Dade College, Miami, Florida

Paul Kern, Green River College, Auburn, Washington
Rachel DeSanto, Hillsborough Community College, Tampa, Florida
Ramon Perez, Northern Virginia Community College, Dumfries, Virginia
Rebecca McNerney, Virginia Commonwealth University, Richmond, Virginia
Richard Roy, Middlesex County College, Edison, New Jersey
Sandra Navarro, Glendale Community College, Glendale, California
Shane Dick, College of Southern Nevada, Las Vegas, Nevada
Sheila Mayne, University of Pennsylvania, Philadelphia, Pennsylvania
Stephen Johnson, Miami Dade College, Florida
Sumeeta Patnaik, Marshall University, Huntington, West Virginia
Summer Webb, International English Center, Colorado

Tom Sugawara, University of Washington, Seattle, Washington
Viviana Simon, Howard Community College, Columbia, Maryland
William Albertson, Drexel University, Philadelphia, Pennsylvania
Yu Bai, Howard Community College, Laurel, Maryland

Middle East
Deborah Abbott, Prince Muhammad Bin Fahd University, Al Khobar, Saudi Arabia
Genie Elatili, Prince Muhammad Bin Fahd University, Al Khobar, Saudi Arabia
Julie Riddlebarger, Khalifa University, United Arab Emirates
Karla Moore, Virginia International Private School, Abu Dhabi, United Arab Emirates
Laila AlQadhi, Kuwait University, Kuwait

FROM THE AUTHORS

Great Writing began in 1998 when three of us were teaching writing and frequently found ourselves complaining about the lack of materials for English language learners. A lot of books talked about writing but did not ask the students to write until the end of a chapter. In essence, the material seemed to be more of a lecture followed by "Now you write an essay." Students were reading a lot but writing little. What was missing was useful sequenced instruction for developing ESL writers by getting them to write.

Each of us had folders with our own original tried-and-true activities, so we set out to combine our materials into a coherent book that would help teachers and students alike. The result was *Great Paragraphs* and *Great Essays*, the original books of the *Great Writing* series. Much to our surprise, the books were very successful. Teachers around the world reached out to us and offered encouragement and ideas. Through the past four editions we have listened to those ideas, improved upon the books, and added four more levels.

We are proud to present this 5th edition of the *Great Writing* series with the same tried-and-true focus on writing and grammar, but with an added emphasis on developing accurate sentences and expanding level-appropriate academic vocabulary.

We thank those who have been involved in the development of this series over the years. In particular for the 5th edition, we would like to thank Laura Le Dréan, Executive Editor; the developmental editors for this edition: Lisl Bove, Eve Yu, Yeny Kim, Jennifer Monaghan, and Tom Jefferies. We will be forever grateful to two people who shaped our original books: Susan Maguire and Kathy Sands-Boehmer. Without all of these professionals, our books would most definitely not be the great works they are right now.

As always, we look forward to hearing your feedback and ideas as you use these materials with your students.

Sincerely,

Keith Folse
April Muchmore-Vokoun
Elena Vestri
David Clabeaux
Tison Pugh

1 | Exploring the Essay

OBJECTIVES
- Analyze the structure of an essay
- Write an effective hook
- Recognize thesis statements
- Make a general and a specific outline

National Geographic Explorer Andrea Reid resurfaces after conducting a Scuba survey of the Solomon Island coral reefs to track the elusive bumphead parrotfish. This research is part of a project that explores how well this endangered fish species is being safeguarded by marine protected areas (MPAs).

FREEWRITE | Look at the photo and read the caption. On a separate piece of paper, write what you think of when you hear the word *exploration*. You can write words, phrases, or sentences.

ELEMENTS OF GREAT WRITING

What Is an Essay?

An **essay** is a collection of paragraphs that presents facts, opinions, and ideas about a topic. Topics can range from the benefits of international travel to an argument for or against wind energy.

Kinds of Essays

There are many kinds of essays. The kind of essay that a writer chooses is often determined by the specific assignment. This book contains examples of five common kinds of essays: **cause-effect, comparison, argument, problem-solution,** and **reaction.** Each of the next five units presents one of these rhetorical styles of essay writing.

Parts of an Essay

An essay has three basic parts: the **introduction**, the **body**, and the **conclusion**. The introduction is the first paragraph, the conclusion is the last paragraph, and the body is made up of the paragraphs in between. One common format of an essay is the five-paragraph essay. In a typical five-paragraph essay, paragraph one introduces the topic and the main idea or thesis statement, paragraphs two through four develop the topic, and paragraph five concludes the essay.

There are pros and cons to wind energy. Wind is an inexpensive, clean, and renewable energy source, but the turbines can be dangerous for birds.

Introduction

The first paragraph, or **introduction**, introduces the topic and includes the **thesis statement**. The thesis states the main idea of the essay (points of development) and often tells what the organization of the information will be. Typically, the thesis statement is found at the end of the introductory paragraph.

Body

Each paragraph in the **body** of the essay includes a **topic sentence** followed by **supporting sentences**. The topic sentence tells the reader the main topic of the paragraph and the controlling idea, or the particular focus the writer will take on the topic. The topic sentence is often the first sentence of a paragraph. Supporting sentences are directly related to the topic sentence. Common supporting sentences give examples, reasons, facts, or more specific information about the topic.

Conclusion

Finally, it is important for an essay to have a good **conclusion**. The introduction and the conclusion often share some of the same ideas in order to remind the reader of the main idea of the essay. After **restating the thesis**, the conclusion may also present a **suggestion, prediction, question**, or **opinion** related to the topic to leave the reader with a strong final impression.

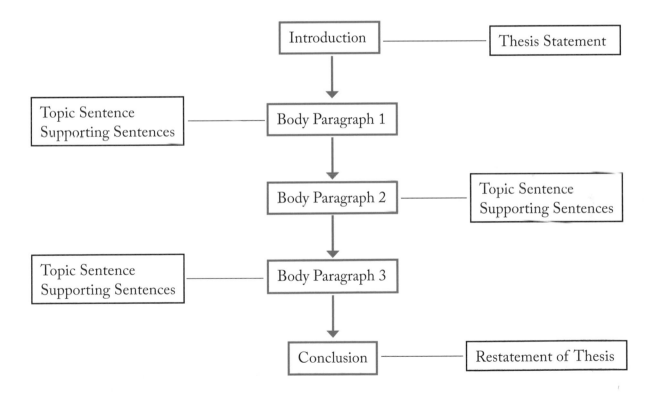

ACTIVITY 1 | Analyzing an essay

Read the essay. Then answer the questions that follow.

> **WORDS TO KNOW** Essay 1.1
>
> **availability:** (n) whether something can be used
> **concept:** (n) an idea; theory; notion
> **obtain:** (v) to get; acquire
>
> **primarily:** (adv) mainly
> **tend to:** (v) to be likely to; to have a tendency toward something

ESSAY 1.1

Shopping for Everyone

1   A college student needs a new laptop. An upcoming wedding requires people in the wedding party to buy formal dresses. A boss asks her accountant for new computer software. These are all everyday purchases. The question is: How can the consumer best **obtain** these items? Previously, there was one technique—shopping in person. Today, however, consumers have various options and can shop based on their preferences. In fact, there are now three main kinds of shopping: in-person, online, and third-party.

2   When thinking about shopping, the method that immediately comes to mind is "in-person" shopping. For millenia[1], consumers have traveled to their local markets to inspect items firsthand. There they could see and touch the merchandise before they purchased it. To understand the popularity of in-person shopping, one just needs to walk into any mall and see the many shoppers who line up in front of cash registers. In-store shopping offers buyers more than just a shopping experience; it offers an opportunity to study items up close using multiple senses.

The Mall of the Emirates Shopping Center in Dubai offers consumers the in-store shopping experience as well as the opportunity to ski.

3   With advances in technology, online shopping has also become a strong consumer option. Online shopping allows customers to compare trends, **availability**, price, and quality without leaving the comfort of their own homes. This, when coupled with the ever-popular free shipping that many manufacturers offer, has made online shopping a valuable tool for customers. It has also given warehouses[2] more power to compete with actual storefronts. Online shopping empowers consumers to buy exactly what they want at the price they are willing to pay without wasting time and energy.

4   Finally, there are third-party personal shopping services, which are used **primarily** in the clothing industry. The **concept** is easy enough: Potential buyers fill out a shopping profile and let the shopping service choose items that fit their profile and preferences. In this day and age, consumers **tend to** spend their time working or running errands and often do not have free time. As a result, third-party shopping services have been created to respond to consumer needs and save people precious time. Why should customers spend time looking for goods and services themselves when they can pay a person or a company to do their shopping for them? After giving a list to this personal shopper, consumers simply wait for the items to arrive at their homes. People who use third-party shoppers tend to have a more generous budget as they must pay for the convenience of not having to look for anything, either in person or online.

5   There are shopping options for everyone. Those who like to browse[3] in person, pick up items, and try them on can do so easily. Those who prefer to shop in the comfort of their own homes have numerous online shopping websites to choose from, and those who trust others to shop for them have access to third-party shopping services. It is amazing to see just how far shopping has come in such a short period of time. It is anyone's guess what the next shopping experience might be.

[1]millenia: thousands of years
[2]warehouse: a large building where products are stored
[3]browse: to look over in a slow, relaxed way

---

1. What is the main purpose of this essay? Begin with *The purpose is...*

   _____

   _____

2. How many paragraphs does this essay have? _____ Which paragraph is the

   introduction? _____ Which paragraph is the conclusion? _____

   Which paragraphs make up the body? _____

3. According to the author of this essay, what are the three types of shopping (the three points of development)?

   _____

4. Can you find a sentence in Paragraph 1 that tells readers what to expect in Paragraphs 2, 3, and 4? Write that sentence here. _____

_____

5. What topic is discussed in Paragraph 2? _____

6. In Paragraph 2, the writer gives proof of the popularity of in-person shopping. What does she describe?

_____

7. Paragraph 4 suggests that third-party shopping is more expensive than the other two types mentioned. Write that sentence here.

_____

_____

8. Look at the last paragraph. Find the sentence that restates the thesis. Write that sentence here.

_____

Hook

The introduction paragraph of an essay often begins with a **hook**. The hook is one or more sentences that get the reader's attention. Just as people use a hook at the end of a fishing line to catch a fish, writers use a hook to catch their readers' attention. Writers may use a famous quote, a broad statement, a question, a statistic, an anecdote or short story, or a historical account of the topic. Look for the hook in the next essay.

ACTIVITY 2 | Analyzing a cause-effect essay

Read the cause-effect essay. Then answer the questions that follow.

WORDS TO KNOW Essay 1.2

be concerned about: (v phr) to worry or feel anxious about
lack of: (n) an absence of; deficiency
lead to: (v) to bring about; cause

overall: (adj) including everything; total
permanently: (adv) forever; always
prevalent: (adj) common; observed frequently
risk: (n) the danger of something; hazard

Cancer Risks

1   In the United States, lung cancer kills more people in one year than all other types of cancer combined. This statistic is shocking, but the good news is that people are now well informed about the **risks** connected to lung cancer. They know that their risk of contracting this terrible disease decreases if they either stop smoking or do not smoke at all. Unfortunately, the same cannot be said about other types of cancer. Many people are not aware that their everyday behavior can **lead to** different forms of cancer. By eating better, exercising regularly, and staying out of the sun, people can reduce their risks of getting cancer.

2   Instead of foods that are good for them, people often eat unhealthy foods, such as burgers, fries, and pizza. These popular foods contain large amounts of saturated fat, which is one of the worst kinds of fat. Although light and fat-free products are constantly being introduced to the consumer market, many people still buy foods that contain fat because they think they taste better. However, eating fatty foods can increase a person's chances of getting some kinds of cancer. In addition, people do not eat as many fresh vegetables and fruits as they used to. Instead, they now eat a lot more processed foods that do not contain natural fiber. **Lack of** fiber in a person's diet can increase the chance of colon cancer. In the past, people with less information about nutrition actually had better diets than people do today. They also had fewer cases of cancer.

3   Many people today are overweight, and being overweight has been connected to some kinds of cancer. Since television sets are now a standard piece of furniture in most living rooms, people spend more time sitting down and mindlessly eating snacks than they did in the past. The first generation of TV watchers started the couch potato[1] boom, and today's couch potatoes are bigger than ever. Health experts warn that being overweight is a risk not only for heart disease but also for certain kinds of cancer. The best way to reach a healthy weight is for people to cut back on[2] the amount of food that they consume and to exercise regularly. It is not possible to do only one of these and lose weight **permanently**. The improved diet must be in conjunction with[3] regular exercise. In the past, people did more physical activity than they do today. For example, most people used to walk to work; now very few people do. In addition, people had jobs that required more physical labor. Now many people have desk jobs that require sitting in front of computers.

---

[1]couch potato: a person who does not move a lot
[2]cut back on: to reduce
[3]in conjunction with: together with

4   Finally, health officials **are concerned about** the dramatic rise in the number of cases of skin cancer. Many societies value a tanned complexion, so on weekends people tend to flock to[4] the beach or swimming pools and lie in the sun. Many of these people do not use a safe sunscreen, and the result is that they get sunburned. Sunburn damages the skin, and repeated damage may lead to skin cancer later in life. Once the damage is done, it cannot be undone. Thus, prevention is important. In the past, people did not lie in direct sunlight for long periods of time, and skin cancer was not as **prevalent** as it is now. People have started to listen to doctors' warnings about this situation, and more and more people are protecting their skin when they are outside. Unfortunately, millions of people already have this potential cancer problem in their skin and may develop cancer later.

5   Cancer has been around since the earliest days of human existence, but only recently has the public been made aware of some of the risk factors involved. Antismoking campaigns can be seen everywhere—on billboards, in television commercials, on the radio, and in newsprint. If the same amount of attention were given to proper diets, exercise, and the right sunscreen, perhaps the number of **overall** cancer cases could be reduced.

[4]flock to: to go in large numbers

People flock to the beach in Lloret de Mar, Spain, to lie in the sun, but sunburn can damage skin and lead to skin cancer. ▲

1. What is the main purpose of this essay? Begin with *The purpose is* ...

   _____

   _____

2. What is the thesis statement of this essay?

   _____

   _____

3. The thesis statement should tell the reader how the essay will be organized. What do you know about the organization of the essay from the thesis statement?

   _____

   _____

4. In Paragraph 2, the writer states that many people eat unhealthy food. What supporting information explains why this food is not healthy?

   _____

   _____

   _____

5. In Paragraph 3, the writer discusses two methods of losing weight that must be done simultaneously. What are they?

   _____

   _____

   _____

6. What is the topic sentence in Paragraph 4? Write it here.

   _____

   _____

7. Reread Paragraphs 1 and 5. What ideas do the introduction and the conclusion share?

   _____

   _____

8. Does the conclusion present a suggestion, a prediction, a question, or an opinion? Does it leave you with a strong final impression?

   _____

   _____

ACTIVITY 3 | Analyzing a comparison essay

Read the comparison essay. Then answer the questions that follow.

WORDS TO KNOW Essay 1.3

appreciate: (v) to value
drawback: (n) a disadvantage; downside
in terms of: (phr) concerning the specific topic

regardless of: (phr) in spite of; despite
selection: (n) a group of things from which to choose

ESSAY 1.3

The Urban and Rural Divide

1   Imagine life in Tokyo, Japan. Now imagine life in a rural Japanese town. Finally, picture life in Cairo, Egypt. Which of these last two places is more different from Tokyo? Many people might mistakenly choose Cairo because it is in a different continent. However, city dwellers[1] all over the world tend to have similar lifestyles, so the bigger differences are found between Tokyo and the rural Japanese town. Urban people and rural people, **regardless of** their country, have distinct lifestyles. Perhaps some of the most notable differences in the lives of these two groups include the degree of friendliness between residents, the pace of life[2], and the variety of available activities.

2   One major difference between growing up in the city and in the country is the degree of friendliness. In large cities, residents often live in huge apartment buildings with hundreds of strangers. These urban apartment dwellers tend to be wary[3] of unknown faces and rarely get to know their neighbors well. The situation in a small town is often just the opposite. Small-town people generally grow up together, attend the same schools, and share the same friends. As a result, rural people are much more likely to treat their neighbors like family and invite them into their homes.

Shibuya Crossing, Tokyo, Japan

Shirakawa-go village, Japan

3   Another difference is the pace of life. In the city, life moves very quickly. The streets reflect this hectic pace and are rarely empty, even late at night. City dwellers appear to be racing to get somewhere important. Life for them tends to be a series of deadlines. In the country, life is much slower. Even during peak[4] hours, traffic jams occur less often than in a city. Stores close in the early evening, and the streets do not come alive until the next morning. The people in small towns or villages seem more relaxed and move in a more leisurely way. The pace of life in these two areas could not be more different.

4   A third difference lies in the way people are able to spend their free time. Although life in the city has its **drawbacks**, city dwellers have a much wider choice of activities that they can participate in. For example, they can go to museums, eat in exotic restaurants, attend concerts, and shop in hundreds of stores. The activities available to people in rural areas, however, are much more limited. It is rare to find museums or unusual restaurants there. Concert tours almost never include stops in country towns. Finally, people who enjoy shopping might be disappointed in the small **selection** of stores.

5   Life in urban areas and life in rural areas vary **in terms of** human interaction, pace of life, and daily activities. None of these differences makes one place better than the other. The places are simply different. Only people who have experienced living in both the city and the country can truly **appreciate** the unique characteristics of each.

[1]dweller: resident
[2]pace of life: the speed at which changes occur
[3]wary: concerned about danger; cautious
[4]peak: the point of greatest activity

1. What is the main purpose of this essay? Begin with *The purpose is…*

_____

_____

2. What is the thesis statement? _____

_____

3. In each paragraph, which type of location is always discussed first—rural or urban?

_____

4. What is the purpose of the first sentence in each body paragraph (2–4)? _____

_____

5. Which paragraph talks about activities in each area? _____

City streets in Shanghai, China

6. In Paragraph 3, the writer contrasts the pace of life in the two areas. Write the supporting sentences for the pace of life in each area.

A. Urban

1. _____

2. _____

3. _____

B. Rural

1. _____

2. _____

3. _____

7. Is there any place in this essay you would like more explanation or detail? If so, where?

_____

_____

ACTIVITY 4 | Analyzing a problem-solution essay

Read the problem-solution essay. Then answer the questions that follow.

ESSAY 1.4

Overcoming the Rising Cost of University Studies

1   A high school diploma is not the end of many students' educational paths. Competition to enter the workforce is fierce[1], and without an advanced degree "in hand," many young people will not succeed in getting adequate employment. With this requirement of a college diploma comes an unforeseen problem: cost. The price tag on studying at a traditional university is growing rapidly, year by year, which leaves many feeling defeated and powerless. Is there a solution to this financial **crisis** for students? Fortunately, more and more options are available for those students who do not **have the means to** attend these universities. One such solution in the United States is attending community college.

2   University costs are rising steadily—both in the United States and in other countries. In the United States alone, the yearly tuition at public universities is approximately $35,000. Does this sound like a lot? Imagine adding in the cost of housing and books. The yearly price tag can be astronomical[2]. This dollar amount is for nonresident students—that is, those students who permanently reside either out of state or out of country. However, even local students pay up to $21,000 yearly. This amount more than triples when one adds on housing and textbooks.

[1]fierce: intense
[2]astronomical: extremely high

Students on a community college campus.

3   Attending a community college is a fine solution to this financial problem. Fees for community college study are half as much as universities. Even better, the quality of education is just as good as, if not better than, a four-year university at a fraction of the cost. While community colleges only offer two-year degrees, many students transfer their credits to a larger university after they complete their coursework. This translates into tens of thousands of dollars saved in the first two years of university study. In addition, community colleges charge less for parking, cafeteria food, and campus health clinic services. No matter how the total bill is calculated or what is included, community colleges are a better value than four-year universities.

4   Community colleges are indeed very different from large universities and may not offer the same social or athletic opportunities. Many people wrongly **assume** that the differences might affect the quality of education. But the quality of the education at community colleges matches that at universities, making the value hard to beat. Beginning at a community college is a perfect solution for students looking to continue on their educational path without going into tremendous debt.

AVERAGE FEES PER YEAR AT U.S. UNIVERSITIES, 2017–18				
	Public 2-year community colleges	Public 4-year colleges (in-state fees)	Public 4-year colleges (out-of-state fees)	Private non-profit 4-year colleges
Tuition and other fees	$3,570	$9,970	$25,620	$34,740
Room and board	$8,400	$10,800	$10,800	$12,210
Total (per year)	$11,970	$20,770	$35,420	$46,950
Source: *College Board, Annual Survey of Colleges*				

1. Review the chart. What is the most expensive type of college or university in the

United States? _____

2. What is the least expensive? What is the approximate total cost difference between the most and least expensive types?

_____

3. Look at the prices of room and board, which refers to housing and food for students. The two-year colleges cost less. What do you think are some reasons for this?

_____

_____

_____

4. What is the purpose of the essay? Begin with *The purpose is...*

_____

_____

5. Complete this simple outline of the essay.

Topic: The Cost of University Studies

  I. Introduction (Paragraph 1)

    Thesis statement: _____

    _____

  II. Body (Paragraphs 2 and 3)

  A. Paragraph 2 topic (PROBLEM): _____

    a. Tuition for nonresidents

    b. _____

  B. Paragraph 3 topic (SOLUTION): _____

    a. Cost of community college

    b. Quality of education

    c. Other services: _____

  III. Conclusion (Paragraph 4)

    Restate thesis

    Opinion: _____

    _____

    _____

SUPPORT

SUPPORT

6. What did you know about this topic before you read this essay? (Check all answers that apply.)

☐ I knew that university education was very expensive in the United States.

☐ I knew that the prices were different for in-state and out-of-state students.

☐ I thought that a university was the only option for higher education in the United States.

☐ I did not know much about university education.

7. What do you think about the writer's solution to the high cost of education? Did the writer make a good argument for community colleges?

_____

_____

8. Can you think of other possible solutions for students who want higher education but cannot afford it?

_____

_____

Writing the Introduction

The **introduction** is the first part of an essay, usually the first paragraph. During the writing process, the introduction does not have to be written first, however. Some writers design and write this part of the essay last or at another point in their writing process.

There are many ways to write an introduction. Some writers begin with a question. Others give background information about the topic. The kind of introduction you choose depends on how you want to present the topic and the kind of essay you decide to write.

What Is in the Introduction?

The introduction for most essays is one paragraph. This paragraph often consists of three parts:

INTRODUCTION =
1. The hook
2. Connecting information
3. The thesis statement

The Hook

As you have learned, the **hook** is the opening statement or statements of an essay. Writers use a hook to catch the readers' attention. If a hook does its job well, readers will stay with the essay and want to read the rest of it. There are many different ways to write a hook:

1. **Ask a question.** If readers want to know the answer to the question, they are "hooked" and will read the essay. For example, a writer might begin an essay about the need for more regulations on technology usage with this question:

   How many people begin their mornings—every day—by checking their cell phones?

2. **Use an interesting observation.**

   European economists are not sleeping well these days.

   This observation makes readers want to know why economists are not sleeping well. It leads to the main idea of the essay, which will highlight the main causes of recession in Europe.

   Here is another example of an observation hook full of interesting details that leads readers to the topic of international trade:

   The average Canadian is proud to be Canadian and can easily talk about the benefits of living in Canada. However, many Canadians drive Japanese or German cars to work every morning. They wear cotton shirts made in Honduras and pants made in Bangladesh. Their dinner salad may contain tomatoes from California and salad dressing from France. Before going to bed, Canadians will most likely watch their favorite TV programs on a Japanese or Korean television.

3. **Use a unique scenario, or description of events, to catch the reader's attention.**

   Traveling at more than one hundred miles an hour, he feels as though he is not moving. He is engulfed in complete silence. For a moment, it is as if he has entered another dimension.

   This vivid description pulls readers in, making them want to find out more. This essay is about the exciting sport of skydiving.

4. **Begin with a famous quote.**

   "I have a dream."

   Many readers may think that this hook will lead into a discussion of Martin Luther King Jr.'s life or his struggles. In fact, this hook begins an essay on the topic of sleep patterns.

5. **Use a surprising or shocking statistic.**

   The South American country of Chile has one of the lowest divorce rates in the world.

   Type II diabetes is the fastest-growing disease in the modern age.

For writing in English, the main idea, or thesis, of an essay is usually in the introduction, but it is generally not the first sentence. The hook is usually the first sentence or the first few sentences. You could begin an essay with a sentence stating the main idea:

This essay will talk about common methods of curbing one's appetite.

or

There are three ways to curb your appetite.

However, in academic writing, beginning with a sentence that plainly states the main idea is <u>not</u> preferred because it gives away the main idea of the essay too soon. Stating the main idea will not grab your readers' attention, so be sure to begin your essay with an interesting hook.

Connecting Information

After the hook, the writer usually writes **connecting information**, which is three to five sentences that connect the hook to the topic. These sentences logically progress to the thesis. The following sentences from Essay 1.2 give connecting information that leads from the hook to the thesis statement:

Hook:
In the United States, lung cancer kills more people in one year than all other types of cancer combined. This statistic is shocking, but the good news is that people are now well informed about the risks connected to lung cancer. They know that their risk of contracting this terrible disease decreases if they either stop smoking or do not smoke at all.

Connecting information:
Unfortunately, the same cannot be said about other types of cancer. Many people are not aware that their everyday behavior can lead to the development of different forms of cancer.

Thesis statement:
By eating better, exercising regularly, and staying out of the sun, people can reduce their risks of cancer.

The Thesis Statement

The **thesis statement** is usually the last part of the introduction. It is usually one sentence. In the thesis statement, the writer tells the reader what to expect in the essay. Basically, there are two kinds of thesis statements—**direct** and **indirect**.

1. **Direct Thesis Statement.** Some writers specifically state their points of development in their thesis statement. Read the following example:

   > The main problems facing this nation are a lack of job opportunities, government corruption, and inadequate university programs for students with limited incomes.

   From this statement, the reader knows that the body of the essay has three main points of development. The first will discuss the lack of job opportunities, the second will talk about government corruption, and the last will talk about the limited number of university programs for low-income students. This kind of thesis statement is called a *direct thesis*.

2. **Indirect Thesis Statement**. Other writers are not so direct. Discussing a similar topic as the previous example, a less direct approach might be:

   > There are three important problems facing the nation today that require immediate attention.

   From this statement, the reader expects to find a discussion of problems in the writer's country. In this case, the reader must continue reading to find the supporting ideas of the argument. This kind of thesis statement is called an *indirect thesis*.

   The introduction from Essay 1.1 is a good example of how the hook, connecting information, and thesis statement capture the reader's interest and provide a clear road map for the information to come.

A college student needs a new laptop. An upcoming wedding requires people in the wedding party to buy — Hook

formal dresses. A boss asks her accountant for new computer software. These are all everyday purchases. The question is: How can the consumer best obtain these items? Previously, there was one technique—shopping in — Connecting information
person. Today, however, consumers have various options, and buyers can shop based on their preferences. In fact, there are now three main kinds of shopping: in-person, — Thesis
online, and third-party.

ACTIVITY 5 | Practice with hooks

This essay begins with the connecting information and thesis statement. First, read the entire essay. Then go back and write two possible hooks that would capture the readers' attention. Share the hooks with your classmates. Explain why you think they will be effective.

> **WORDS TO KNOW** Essay 1.5
>
> **countless:** (adj) numerous; unlimited number **roughly:** (adv) approximately
> **crucial:** (adj) essential; very important

Jim Henson and his Muppets

ESSAY 1.5

The Role of Advertising in Society

1 Hook 1: _____

_____

Hook 2: _____

_____

Are we being exposed to too much advertising? Parents seem to think so. Many mothers and fathers are worried about the impact that advertising might have on young minds. Whether it is accepted or not, advertising affects each and every person it touches. When one looks at this issue critically, however, it is clear that advertising can benefit society in many ways.

2   The first reason advertising benefits society is the sheer size of the industry. In the United States alone, the advertising industry employs **roughly** 200,000 people. This number has grown consistently since 2001. Experts predict that global advertising spending will reach over $700 billion by 2020. The economic benefits of advertising cannot be denied. Individuals should celebrate this economic growth as it impacts many people.

3   Advertising also drives the creativity of a nation. Ask anyone, and he or she will be able to recall, in clear detail, his or her favorite advertisement and its creative features. It is also not uncommon to hear a group of friends discussing their favorite ads from their childhoods. Many artists work in the advertising industry, and their work influences the cultural narrative of society. For instance, Jim Henson, the creative genius behind The Muppets, began his career in advertising.

4   Advertising also has an important role in raising public awareness. People may wrongly assume that advertising is only about marketing and selling products. However, there are many instances of advertisers involved in public awareness campaigns. As society tries to deal with disturbing current events, advertisers can get people to think about the problems by mentioning them in commercials and print ads. In the past, for example, advertisements discussing the dangers of smoking or the importance of wearing a seatbelt saved **countless** lives.

5   Some people complain that advertising is responsible for information overload and can have negative psychological effects, especially on children. However, advertising can be used as a learning tool. Parents can use ads to teach their children the **crucial** life skill of critical thinking, giving them the opportunity to challenge the information they are given. Advertising is everywhere, and both adults and children must learn to evaluate the messages that these advertisements are sending.

6   Advertising has brought society many benefits, both financial and educational. Historically, it has been an extremely important industry. No, not every group should be exposed to all advertisements all the time. However, the industry should be celebrated for the way it adds color and creativity to the world.

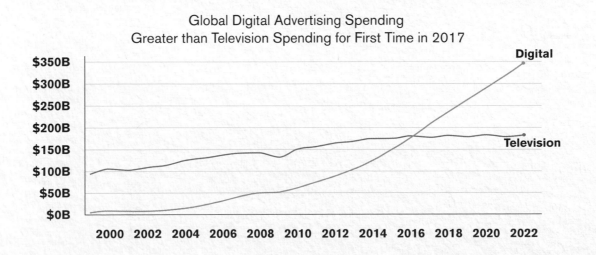

Global Digital Advertising Spending
Greater than Television Spending for First Time in 2017

ACTIVITY 6 | Practice with thesis statements

Answer these questions about the thesis statement in Essay 1.5.

1. What is the thesis statement in the essay?

_____

_____

2. Is this a direct or indirect thesis statement? _____

3. Rewrite the thesis statement using the alternative form.

_____

_____

_____

ACTIVITY 7 | Understanding graphs

Answer these questions about the graph on page 23.

1. Approximately how much was spent on digital advertising in 2017? How much is expected to be spent in 2020?

_____

2. How much is expected to be spent on television advertising in 2020? How does that compare with current spending?

_____

3. In addition to digital and television, what other types of advertising can you think of?

_____

ACTIVITY 8 | More practice with hooks

This essay begins with the connecting information and thesis. First, read the entire essay. Then go back and write a hook that would capture the readers' attention. Share it with your classmates. Explain why you think it will be effective.

> **WORDS TO KNOW** Essay 1.6
>
> **fundamental:** (adj) essential; very important   **mediate:** (v) to help both sides in negotiations reach an agreement

The Truth about Coaches and Business Managers

1   Hook: _____

_____

Coaches often work outdoors while business managers tend to stay in offices. Coaches train athletes' bodies, while managers are focused on their business. These differences, however, pale in comparison[1] to the similarities shared by the two professions, for the main functions of athletic team coaches and business managers are very closely related.

2   One of the most **fundamental** similarities between athletic team coaches and business managers is the task of leading the team members or employees. Coaches are responsible for training their athletes and focusing on each individual's strengths and weaknesses. Coaches also give directions to their players to improve their performance and commonly give feedback after a game. Similarly, business managers are responsible for the proper training of their employees. Managers use their people skills to ensure that each worker is put in the job that suits his or her abilities best. In addition, managers typically give periodic reviews of their employees as feedback on their job performance.

3   Another important similarity between the two professions is the ability to solve problems between teammates or employees. Athletes tend to be very competitive, and often this competitiveness leads to arguments in practice and during games. Coaches know that this behavior is not productive in leading the team to victory, so they often act as intermediaries[2]. They listen to both sides and usually come up with words of wisdom or advice to straighten out the problem. In the same way, a manager is often asked to **mediate** between two or more employees who might not be getting along in the office. Managers know that teamwork is vital to productivity, so they are trained to make sure that the workplace runs smoothly.

[1]pale in comparison: to be inferior to
[2]intermediary: a person who acts as the communicator between people or groups

4 Finally, both coaches and managers must represent their subordinates to higher management. Many social groups function as hierarchies[3], and the locker room and office are no different. Coaches are regularly asked to report to the team owners with updates on the season. They write up reports to keep the owners informed about who is doing well, who is injured, and who is not performing up to par[4]. In addition, they serve as the players' spokespersons. If players have a particular problem related to something other than their athletic performance, it is usually the coaches who end up speaking with the owners on the players' behalf. Like coaches, business managers are the links between the executives and lower-level employees. Business managers are given the tasks of overseeing employees and serving as go-betweens. Top management wants to remain aware of what is happening in the company, but they usually do not have the time to deal with such details. Business managers, therefore, serve as spokespeople to both ends of the hierarchy.

5 On the surface, the two occupations seem completely unrelated. The coach tends to work in an informal environment such as an outdoor field or a gym. Business managers are used to interacting with others in more formal spaces such as an office or a boardroom. Upon further inspection, however, these two occupations are very closely related. Both coaches and managers are the glue that holds the members of their teams together.

[3]hierarchy: an organization from higher to lower by rank, social status, or function
[4]up to par: satisfactory or up to a given standard

ACTIVITY 9 | More practice with thesis statements

Answer these questions about the thesis statement in Essay 1.6.

1. What is the thesis statement in the essay?

_____

_____

2. Is this a direct or indirect thesis? _____
Give the reason for your answer.

_____

3. Rewrite the thesis statement using the alternative form.

_____

_____

_____

Writing the Body: Outlining

The body of an essay is its main part. It usually consists of three or four paragraphs between the introduction and the conclusion. The body follows a plan of organization that the writer usually determines before he or she starts writing. This organization varies depending on the kind of essay the writer is writing.

Writers can write the organizational plan of an essay in an **outline**. There are different levels of outlining. A **general** or **simple outline** (see Activity 4) includes the main points, while a **specific** or **detailed outline** includes notes on even the smallest pieces of information that will go into the essay. It is much easier to write an essay from a specific outline than from a general outline. However, most writers start with a general outline first and then add details.

Here are a general outline and a specific outline for Essay 1.6. Compare the two.

GENERAL OUTLINE	SPECIFIC OUTLINE
I. Introduction	I. Introduction
A. Hook: Pose a question	A. Hook: Which is harder, working in business or working in sports?
B. Connecting information	B. Connecting information: They work in different places and focus on different jobs.
C. Thesis: Similarities in coaches' and managers' jobs	C. Thesis: The two professions share many similarities, because the main functions of athletic team coaches and business managers are very closely related.
II. Body	II. Body

A. Similarity 1: Leading the athletes and employees	A. Similarity 1: Leading the athletes and employees
	1. Coaches train athletes
	  a. Focus on strengths and weaknesses
	  b. Give feedback
	2. Managers train employees
	  a. Put employees in jobs that fit them best
	  b. Perform job reviews

B. Similarity 2: Solving problems	B. Similarity 2: Solving problems
	1. Coaches listen to athletes
	  a. Stop arguments
	  b. Act as go-betweens
	2. Managers mediate in office
	  a. Stress importance of teamwork with employees
	  b. Get officemates to cooperate

C. Similarity 3: Representing the athletes and employees	C. Similarity 3: Representing the athletes and employees
	1. Coaches to owners
	  a. Give updates to owners
	  b. Discuss athletes' problems
	2. Managers to CEOs
	  a. Maintain control on behalf of the bosses
	  b. Update the CEOs on employee issues

III. Conclusion: Focus on maintaining communication	III. Conclusion: Both roles are fundamental in improving communication and keeping the team together.

ACTIVITY 10 | Making a general outline

Here is a general outline for Essay 1.1. Read the essay again and complete this outline.

Title: _____

  I. Introduction (Paragraph 1)

   A. Hook: Give a few shopping scenarios

   B. Connecting information

   C. Thesis statement: _____

   _____

  II. Body (Paragraphs 2–4)

   A. Paragraph 2 topic sentence: When thinking about shopping, the method that immediately comes to mind is "in-person" shopping.

   B. Paragraph 3 topic sentence: _____

   _____

   C. Paragraph 4 topic sentence: _____

   _____

  III. Conclusion (Paragraph 5)

   A. Restatement of thesis

   B. Prediction

ACTIVITY 11 | Making a specific outline

Here is a specific outline for the same essay on types of shopping. Reread Essay 1.1 and complete this outline.

Title: _____

I. Introduction (Paragraph 1)

   A. Hook: _____

      _____

   B. Connecting information: _____

      _____

   C. Thesis statement: _____

      _____

II. Body

   A. Paragraph 2

      1. Topic sentence (Shopping type #1): _____

      _____

      2. Supporting ideas

         a. History of in-person shopping

         b. _____

SUPPORT

In-person shopping is just one of several options

B. Paragraph 3

    1. Topic sentence (Shopping type #2): _____

    _____

    2. Supporting ideas

        a. Benefits to shoppers: Without leaving home, can compare

            (1) _____

            (2) availability

            (3) price

            (4) _____

        b. Benefit to producers: can sell merchandise from a warehouse

        c. Saving time and energy

C. Paragraph 4

    1. Topic sentence (Shopping type #3): _____

    _____

    2. Supporting ideas

        a. Steps

            (1) _____

            (2) Guidelines followed by shopping service

III. Conclusion (Paragraph 5)

    A. Review of the three types

    B. Prediction: It is anyone's guess what the next shopping experience might be.

SUPPORT

SUPPORT

Writing the Conclusion

When you write a conclusion, follow these guidelines:

1. Let the reader know that this is the conclusion. You can mark the conclusion with a transition or connector that tells the reader that this is the final paragraph of the essay. Here are some examples:

    In conclusion,   From the information given,   To summarize,*

    *For a more complete list, see *Connectors* in the *Writer's Handbook*.

    Sometimes the first sentence of the conclusion restates the thesis or main idea of the essay:

    Thesis: All new parents will encounter a number of problems.
    Start of the conclusion: As previously noted, there are numerous problems that new parents face today.

2. Do not introduce new information in the conclusion. The conclusion should help the reader to reconsider the main ideas that you have given in the essay. Any new information in the concluding paragraph will sound like a continuation of the body of the essay.

3. Write the best conclusion for the kind of essay you are writing. The essay type may determine the way you end the essay; however, the following ideas can be helpful for any essay.

    a. The final sentence or sentences of an essay often give a suggestion, a prediction, a question, or an opinion about the topic of the essay.

    Suggestion: In order for young people to successfully learn a language, parents should encourage them at an early age.
    Prediction: If more young people were bilingual, perhaps they would better understand the complex world around them.
    Question: What could be more beneficial than being raised bilingual?
    Opinion: Learning a second language at an early age is, in effect, a smart choice.

    b. Sometimes the final sentence or sentences simply say that the issue has been discussed with so many strong, persuasive facts that the answer to the issue is now clear.

    Once aware of this information, any reader would agree that bilingual education is an excellent educational opportunity.

WRITER'S NOTE Checking the First and Last Paragraphs

After you write your essay, read the introductory paragraph and the concluding paragraph. The conclusion should reinforce the main idea presented in the thesis.

BUILDING BETTER VOCABULARY

WORDS TO KNOW

appreciate (v) AW
assume (v) AW
availability (n) AW
be concerned about (v phr)
concept (n) AW
countless (adj)
crisis (n)
crucial (adj) AW

drawback (n)
fundamental (adj) AW
have the means to (v phr)
in terms of (phr)
lack of (n)
lead to (v)
mediate (v) AW
obtain (v) AW

overall (adj) AW
permanently (adv)
prevalent (adj)
primarily (adv) AW
regardless of (phr)
risk (n)
roughly (adv)
selection (n) AW
tend to (v)

AW This icon indicates that the word is on an academic word list.

ACTIVITY 12 | Word associations

Circle the word or phrase that is more closely related to the bold word or phrase on the left.

1. assume	dinner	idea
2. drawback	advantage	disadvantage
3. fundamental	belief	citizens
4. have the means to	impossible	possible
5. in terms of	related to	without
6. lack of	including	without
7. prevalent	uncommon	common
8. regardless of	the book	the situation
9. selection	expensive	multiple
10. tend to	likely	unlikely

ACTIVITY 13 | Collocations

Fill in the blank with the word or phrase that most naturally completes the phrase.

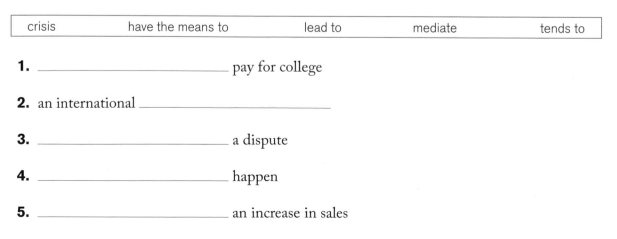

crisis	have the means to	lead to	mediate	tends to

1. _____ pay for college

2. an international _____

3. _____ a dispute

4. _____ happen

5. _____ an increase in sales

| countless | crucial | obtain | permanently | roughly |

6. _____ reasons

7. _____ damaged

8. _____ an advanced degree

9. _____ for success

10. _____ 100 kilos in weight

ACTIVITY 14 | Word forms

Complete each sentence with the correct word form. Use the correct form of the verbs.

NOUN	VERB	ADJECTIVE	ADVERB	SENTENCES
appreciation	appreciate	appreciative	appreciatively	**1.** He sent his adviser flowers as a sign of his _____. **2.** People who _____ the simple things tend to be happy.
availability		available		**3.** The doctor is only _____ on Tuesdays and Thursdays. **4.** The _____ of public transportation makes New York easy to navigate.
fundamentals		fundamental	fundamentally	**5.** His experiment will not work because it is _____ flawed. **6.** One of the _____ elements of biology is osmosis.
primary		primary	primarily	**7.** The professor's _____ message was misunderstood. **8.** The foreign population of the United Arab Emirates is _____ Indian.
risk	risk	risky		**9.** Texting while driving is _____. **10.** The _____ of fire is great because of the recent droughts.

ACTIVITY 15 | Vocabulary in writing

Choose five words from Words to Know. Write a complete sentence with each word.

1. _____

2. _____

3. _____

4. _____

5. _____

BUILDING BETTER SENTENCES

ACTIVITY 16 | Editing

Look at the underlined words. If there is an error, write the correction above the word.

1. More than 42 million <u>family</u> (families) in the United States face the daily challenge of caring for their <u>elders</u>.

2. The problems <u>occurrence</u> when the storm <u>suddenly</u> changed course.

3. Many people do not know that the Amazon river <u>dolphins</u> are <u>pink</u>.

4. In terms of job <u>security</u>, the Highland Company is one of the most <u>stability</u>.

5. Queen Elizabeth I is considered one of the <u>greatest</u> monarchs in British <u>historical</u>.

6. Is it <u>true</u> that Japanese people have such long life spans because of their <u>diet?</u>

ACTIVITY 17 | Writing sentences

Read the pairs of words. Write an original sentence using the words listed.

1. (politician/years) _Our local politician has been in office for eight years._

2. (roughly/risk) _____

3. (lack of/lead to) _____

4. (prevalent/crisis) _____

5. (assume/permanently) _____

6. (overall/tend to) _____

Combining Sentences

Some writers like to keep their sentences short because they feel that if they write longer and more complicated sentences, they are more likely to make mistakes. However, longer sentences connect ideas, and this makes it easier for the reader to understand. Study these sentences. The important information is circled.

(Residents went) to the (town hall meeting.)

Residents wanted to (protest) a (proposal.)

The proposal was for (a new parking structure.)

The most important information from each sentence can be used to create longer, more coherent sentences. Notice that a word form may change, but no ideas are changed or omitted. There is usually more than one way to combine sentences. Both of these sentences are good ways to combine the shorter sentences:

Residents went to the town hall meeting to protest the proposed new parking structure.

The residents wanted to protest the proposed new parking structure, so they went to the town hall meeting.

ACTIVITY 18 | Combining sentences

Combine the ideas into one sentence. You may change the word forms, but do not change or omit any ideas. There may be more than one answer.

1. There is another chore.
The chore is in the household.
Many people dislike this chore.
The chore is washing dishes.

_____

2. No one got an A on the final exam.
It was in the class.
The class taught history.

_____

3. The manager was reviewing her presentation.
At the same time, her assistant was setting up the technology.
This happened in the room.
The room was for conferences.

WRITING

Understanding the Writing Process: The Seven Steps

There are many ways to write, but most good writers follow certain steps in the writing process.

Step 1: **Choose a topic.** Ideally the topic should be something that interests you.

Step 2: **Brainstorm.** Write down as many ideas as you can about your chosen topic; you will move things around and change ideas as you reach Step 3.

Step 3: **Outline.** Once you have a topic, it is time to put your ideas into a logical format. Write an outline to help you organize how you will present your ideas.

Step 4: **Write the first draft.** Use the information from your brainstorming session and your outline to write a first draft. At this stage, do not worry about errors in your writing. Focus on putting your ideas into sentences.

Step 5: **Get feedback from a peer.** The more feedback you have, the better. Your classmates can help you with the content and organization of your paper, as can your instructor.

Step 6: **Reread, rethink, rewrite.** Based on the feedback you receive, consider making some changes.

Step 7: **Proofread the final draft.** Review the final paper before you turn it in. Be sure it is typed, double-spaced, and free of any grammatical and spelling errors.

For more detailed information on these steps, see *Steps in the Writing Process* in the *Writer's Handbook*.

ACTIVITY 19 | Essay writing practice

Write an essay on one of the following suggested topics. Depending on the topic that you choose, you may need to do some research. Use at least two of the vocabulary words or phrases presented in the unit. Underline these words and phrases in your essay. Before you write, be sure to refer to the seven steps in the writing process.

If you need ideas for phrasing, see *Useful Words and Phrases* in the *Writer's Handbook*.

Additional Topics for Writing

Here are five ideas for writing. Follow your teacher's instructions and choose one or more topics to write about. Exchange your first draft with a partner and use Peer Editing Form 1 in the *Writer's Handbook* to help you comment on your partner's essay. Then revise your essay based on your partner's feedback.

TOPIC 1: Look at the photo on pages 2–3 and reread your freewrite. Describe a place or a subject you have explored and how the experience affected you.

TOPIC 2: Write an essay about different types of teachers. Choose three types and focus on their teaching styles.

TOPIC 3: Many recent developments in technology, such as the smartphone or tablet computer, have changed our lives. Write an essay in which you discuss the effects of one recent technological invention on society.

TOPIC 4: There are different theories about the best personality that a business leader should have. Some people believe that leaders should be assertive. They need to show a high confidence level to their workers in order to motivate them. Others insist that humility is a much better personality trait for business leaders. They argue that humility empowers the employees more because the boss does not take credit for achievements. Write an essay in which you defend one of these points of view.

TOPIC 5: Write about a movie or book that you particularly like. Why was it so good? Give three reasons. Give specific examples to support your ideas.

TEST PREP

> **TIP**
>
> Organize your ideas before you write. First make a list of ideas. Then review the list, placing a number next to each idea, from most important to least important. In this way, if you do not have enough time to complete your writing, you will be sure that the most relevant information will be included in your essay.

You should spend about 40 minutes on this task. Write a five-paragraph essay in response to the following topic:

What are the benefits of knowing a second language?

Be sure to begin your essay with an effective hook. Use a variety of sentence types: from simple to more complex. Write at least 250 words.

2 | Cause-Effect Essays

OBJECTIVES
- Write a cause-effect essay
- Use connectors in cause-effect writing
- Understand noun clauses

Rivers drain into the Java Sea from the north coast of West Java, Indonesia. Monsoon rains flood the rivers, resulting in floodwaters that are full of sediment (the rocks, sand, and dirt that settle on the river bottom). The floodwaters discolor the Java Sea as they enter it along the coastline.

FREEWRITE | Look at the photo and read the caption. On a separate piece of paper, write what comes to mind about this or another natural cause-effect relationship.

ELEMENTS OF GREAT WRITING

What Is a Cause-Effect Essay?

A **cause-effect essay** explains the relationship between an event and its consequences, or between actions and results. For example, if too much commercial fishing is allowed in the North Atlantic Ocean (action), the fish population in some areas may diminish or disappear (result). Cause-effect essays can be informative, analytical, and insightful. In addition to being able to write a cause-effect essay, you should know how to write a single paragraph discussing a cause, an effect, or both to be included in a longer essay you are writing.

In this unit, you will study two kinds of cause-effect essays. In one method, the focus is on the causes of something. This is called the **focus-on-causes** method. Essays that focus on causes answer the question *Why does something happen?* In the second method, the focus is on the effects or results of a cause. This is called the **focus-on-effects** method. Essays that focus on effects answer the question *What happens when or if. . . ?*

Imagine that your instructor gives you the following writing topic: quitting a job. You have the choice of using the focus-on-causes method or the focus-on-effects method.

Focus-on-causes: You can choose to write an essay on why people quit their jobs and brainstorm possible reasons they may have for doing so, such as distance from home or lack of benefits. Each paragraph would contain a different cause.

Focus-on-effects: On the other hand, you may want to emphasize the effects of quitting a job—perhaps detailing the emotional and financial consequences—in your body paragraphs. In this case, each paragraph would address one effect.

ACTIVITY 1 | Analyzing a cause-effect essay

Read the cause-effect essay (focus on causes). Then answer the questions that follow.

WORDS TO KNOW Essay 2.1

consequence: (n) a negative result
exemplify: (v) to represent, typify
irresponsible: (adj) careless; not wise about one's behavior or obligations

maintain: (v) to make something continue
motive: (n) a cause for doing something
somewhat: (adv) slightly, a bit

The Truth Behind Lying

1   Most children are taught the virtue[1] of honesty from fairy tales and other stories. The well-known story of Pinocchio, who begins life as a puppet, teaches the importance of telling the truth. Every time Pinocchio lies, his nose grows longer and longer. Another story that **exemplifies** how lying can lead to ruin is the one about the boy who "cried wolf." In the end, he loses all his sheep as well as the trust of his fellow villagers due to his lies. In the United States, young children learn the tale of six-year-old George Washington, who bravely admits to his father that he cut down a cherry tree. His honesty earns him his father's praise and respect. These types of stories show children that "honesty is the best policy." Still, if this is the case, then why do so many people lie? The fact is that people lie for many reasons.

2   One reason people lie is to minimize a mistake. While it is true that everyone does something wrong from time to time, some people do not have the courage to admit their errors because they are afraid they will be blamed or judged. For example, students might lie to their teachers about unfinished homework. They might say that they left the work at home when, in fact, they did not do the work at all. These students do not want to get in trouble or seem **irresponsible**, so they make up an excuse—a lie—to save face[2].

3   Another reason people lie is to get out of situations that they do not want to be in or cannot manage. For example, if a company decides to have a weekend meeting, one of the managers might not feel like attending. She may call her boss and give this excuse: "I've been fighting off a cold all week, and I cannot risk getting the others sick. I'll be sure to get all of the notes on Monday." When individuals do not want to admit the truth and then face the **consequences**, they lie to avoid difficulties.

[1]virtue: behavior showing high moral standards
[2]save face: to retain respect; avoid humiliation

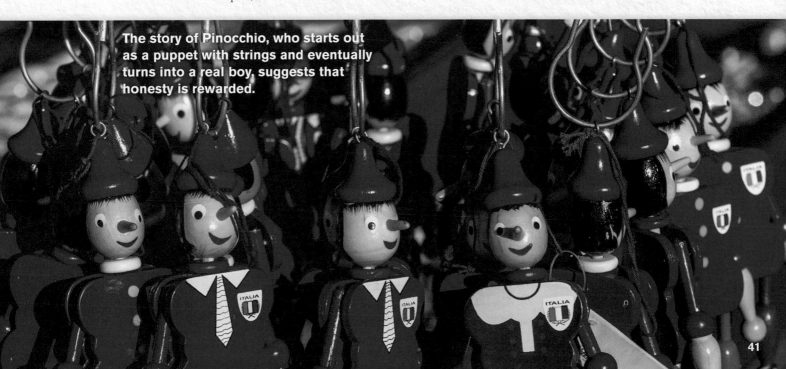

The story of Pinocchio, who starts out as a puppet with strings and eventually turns into a real boy, suggests that honesty is rewarded.

4   In contrast, some people might tell a "white lie" when they do not want to hurt someone else's feelings. For example, if a good friend shows up with an unflattering new haircut, one could be truthful and say, "That haircut looks awful. What were you thinking?" A more gentle response is to say, "It's very original! It suits you." These types of lies are generally not considered negative or wrong. In fact, many people who have told the truth to loved ones, only to see the negative reaction, wish they *had* told a white lie. White lies can be useful in **maintaining** good relationships.

5   A **somewhat** different reason for lying has to do with self-protection. Parents, particularly those with young children, may teach their children to use this type of "protective" lie in certain circumstances. What should children do if a stranger calls while the parents are out? Many parents teach their children to explain that their mother and father are too busy to come to the phone at that time. In this situation, protective lying can mean greater safety.

6   People lie for many reasons, both good and bad. Lying to keep the peace or to stay safe can have positive results. However, lying to stay out of trouble can lead to more trouble in the end. Understanding the **motives** behind the impulse[3] to lie might minimize this habit of lying.

[3]impulse: a strong desire to act

---

1. What is the main purpose of this essay? Begin with *The purpose is…*

   _____

2. What is the thesis statement? _____

   _____

3. What kind of hook does the writer use in this essay? Circle the best answer.

   question   interesting observation   scenario   quote   other

4. Reread the introduction. Between the hook and the thesis statement, the writer uses connecting information. Write that sentence or sentences here.

   _____

   _____

5. In Paragraph 4, the idiom *a white lie* is used in the topic sentence but is not defined. Write your own definition of a white lie. _____

   _____

6. In Paragraph 5, the author supports the topic sentence by giving an example of a dangerous situation. What example does the author give?

_____

_____

7. In the space below, write your own concluding sentence.

_____

_____

_____

ACTIVITY 2 | Analyzing a cause-effect essay

Read the cause-effect essay (focus on effects). Then answer the questions that follow.

WORDS TO KNOW Essay 2.2

correlation: (n) a connection between things
fatigued: (adj) extremely tired or exhausted
imply: (v) to suggest something indirectly

in the meantime: (phr) the period between two events; meanwhile
substantial: (adj) large, considerable
thrive: (v) to grow strong and healthy

ESSAY 2.2

Insomnia: Some Surprising Effects

1   A colleague yawns[1] all day. A father is impatient with his toddler. A professor cannot concentrate on her lecture. These three things, while seemingly different, have one thing in common: They are typical results of lack of sleep. Insomnia, the inability to fall asleep or stay asleep, affects a **substantial** number of individuals. Although insomnia is a fairly common problem, most people do not know about the dangerous effects it can have on the heart.

2   For one, insomnia can cause an increase in blood pressure, according to Dr. Alexandros N. Vgontzas, a specialist at the Sleep Research and Treatment Center at the Pennsylvania State College of Medicine. The heart **thrives** when blood pressure is normal. If it is too high, the heart suffers. High blood pressure can lead to stroke, heart attack, or heart failure. Recent studies have found that "insomniacs who sleep less than five hours a night are five times more likely to develop high blood pressure than sound sleepers who get enough rest." (Boyles, Salynn) In other words, lack of sleep can lead to high blood pressure, making insomnia an indirect cause of heart problems.

This information names the author of the article where this quote was found. Always include the specific Web address at the end of your essay to show the proper source.

[1]yawn: to involuntarily open one's mouth and inhale deeply due to tiredness or boredom

3   Insomnia is also suspected to cause a higher heart rate. When the heart beats too rapidly, the strain can be very dangerous. Although scientists have not found a direct cause-effect relationship between insomnia and heart failure, there is definitely a **correlation** between the two. The less a person sleeps, the higher the risk for heart problems. A lower heart rate **implies** better cardiovascular[2] health. Athletes, for example, have a normal resting heart rate of approximately 40 beats per minute whereas the average, less fit adult has a rate between 60 and 100. It is believed that people with insomnia have higher heart rates, and perhaps this is what leads to their increased risk of heart problems.

4   People who suffer from insomnia often make unhealthy lifestyle choices, and these choices can affect heart health. For instance, many insomniacs are so **fatigued** during the day that they do not have the energy to eat healthily. They often find themselves eating fast food and other unhealthy snacks instead of cooking nutritious alternatives. Healthy lifestyle choices also include proper exercise, which the typical insomniac avoids. While this avoidance of exercise is understandable because of the insomniac's lack of energy, it contributes to heart problems.

5   Insomnia is a well-known condition that most people have experienced at least once in their lifetimes. However, those individuals who suffer from chronic[3] insomnia are at a greater risk of heart problems. The scientific community continues to research the connection between insomnia and heart problems. **In the meantime**, insomniacs must remain aware of the potential dangers that their sleep patterns can have on their heart health.

Boyles, Salynn. (2009, April 1). Insomnia Raises Risk of High Blood Pressure. Retrieved from https://www.webmd.com/hypertension-high-blood-pressure/news/20090401/insomnia-raises-risk-of-high-blood-pressure#1

[2]cardiovascular: of or relating to the heart and blood vessels
[3]chronic: persisting for a long time or constantly recurring

One traditional way to fall asleep when suffering from insomnia is to count sheep.

1. What is the main purpose of this essay? Begin with *The purpose is...*

   _____

   _____

2. Reread the thesis statement. Is it direct or indirect? _____

3. Write the topic sentence of each body paragraph. For each, circle the word(s) that tell you what the paragraph will focus on.

   Paragraph 2: _____

   _____

   Paragraph 3: _____

   _____

   Paragraph 4: _____

   _____

4. In Paragraph 2, the writer explains that high blood pressure is a negative effect of insomnia. What evidence does the writer give to show the dangers of high blood pressure?

   _____

   _____

5. Read the following sentence: *Daily or even weekly exercise would lessen the chance of heart problems.* In which paragraph does this sentence belong? ___ _____

6. Read the conclusion. Which sentence restates the thesis? Write it here.

   _____

   _____

WRITER'S NOTE Crediting Outside Sources

The more advanced your writing, the more likely you are to use outside sources. If you searched for information from an outside source such as a website, you must show where that information came from (a Web address or URL). Even if your online research is a simple dictionary definition, make sure that you include the name of the website and its URL. Remember: If the information is NOT your own, you must give credit to the source.

Developing a Cause-Effect Essay

ACTIVITY 3 | Outlining a cause-effect essay

Complete the following two outlines with a partner. The first one outlines the causes of bullying behavior, and the second one outlines the effects of bullying. Use your imagination, knowledge of the topic, and understanding of essay organization. Use the thesis statements and topic sentences to help you complete the outlines.

Focus on Causes

Topic: The causes of bullying behavior

I. Introduction (Paragraph 1)

    A. Hook: _____

    _____

    B. Thesis statement: Bullying behavior can occur for many reasons, some of which are

    _____

    _____

II. Body

    A. Paragraph 2 (Cause 1) topic sentence: Teens often begin bullying because they want to feel in control.

        1. Bullying gives young people an identity.

        2. Bullying makes them feel powerful—they feel bigger when they make others feel small.

        3. _____

    B. Paragraph 3 (Cause 2) topic sentence: _____

    _____

        1. In many families, both parents work outside the home.

        2. Parents often do not have time to pay attention to their children's needs.

        3. Parents may not be aware that their children are exhibiting aggressive behavior outside the home.

(SUPPORT)

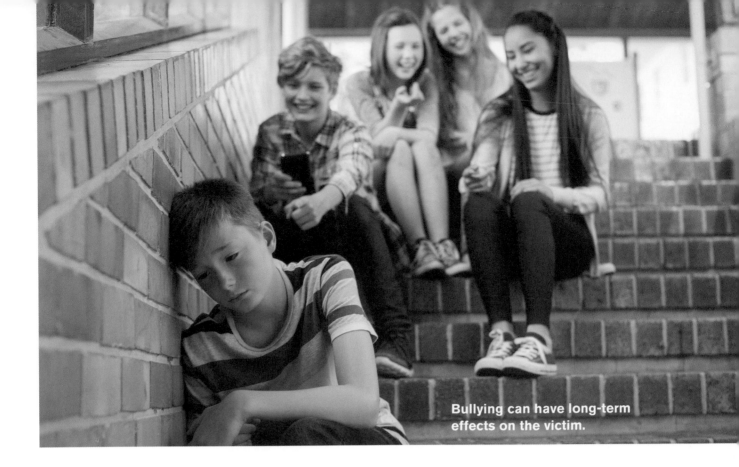

Bullying can have long-term effects on the victim.

C. Paragraph 4 (Cause 3) topic sentence: _____

_____

1. They feel entitled to anything and everything.

2. They have no set rules, boundaries, or punishment.

3. They never hear the word *no*.

III. Conclusion (Paragraph 5) (restated thesis): _____

_____

_____

Focus on Effects

Topic: The effects of bullying on the victim

I. Introduction (Paragraph 1)

   A. Hook: _____

      _____

   B. Thesis statement: When young people are bullied, the effects can be serious.

II. Body

   A. Paragraph 2 (Effect 1) topic sentence: Students who are bullied tend to withdraw from society.

      1. They often stop communicating with parents and friends.

      2. They want to hide this embarrassing situation.

      3. _____

   B. Paragraph 3 (Effect 2) topic sentence: Students lose self-esteem.

      1. They start questioning their own personalities, thinking that maybe they deserve this bad treatment.

      2. _____

      3. Their outlook on life may become darker and darker as the bullying continues.

   C. Paragraph 4 (Effect 3) topic sentence: If teens become damaged by the bullying, they may start exhibiting dangerous behavior.

      1. This behavior takes the focus away from the bullying.

      2. They might think about a plan of revenge.

      3. _____

III. Conclusion (Paragraph 5) (restated thesis): _____

_____

SUPPORT

SUPPORT

SUPPORT

ACTIVITY 4 | Writing supporting information

Follow these steps.

1. The following essay includes an introduction, three topic sentences, and a conclusion. Develop each body paragraph with supporting information. You may write on a separate piece of paper.

2. After you finish, compare your supporting information with that of other students.

WORDS TO KNOW Essay 2.3

compelling: (adj) generating interest
currently: (adv) at the present time; now
distinguish: (v) to see or understand differences
familiarize: (v) to learn about; become acquainted with

have a point: (v phr) to say something that is important or true
inappropriate: (adj) not suitable for the situation
undergo: (v) to go through; experience

ESSAY 2.3

Television at Its Worst

1   Mr. Stevenson has just come home from an extremely tiring day at work. The first thing he does, after taking off his tie and shoes, is fall backward onto the couch and turn on the television. Does this sound like a normal routine? It should because Mr. Stevenson's actions are repeated by millions around the world. People use television to relax and to forget about their daily troubles. However, what started out decades[1] ago as an exciting, new type of family entertainment is **currently** being blamed for serious problems, especially in children. Many researchers now claim that too much television is not good for kids. They **have a point**; watching too much TV often does have negative effects on children and adolescents[2].

[1]decade: a period of ten years
[2]adolescent: a teenager

Television: How much is too much?

2   One negative effect of TV on children is laziness. _____

_____

_____

_____

_____

3   Another problem children have when they watch too much TV is difficulty **distinguishing** between what is real and what is not. _____

_____

_____

_____

_____

4   Finally, television may lead children to _____

_____

_____

_____

_____

5   Television has **undergone** major changes over the years and now includes more and more programs that are **inappropriate** for children. However, there is also a lot of high-quality educational content available, especially on public television channels. These shows can be **compelling** teaching tools. It is up to parents to **familiarize** themselves with the options and monitor their children's viewing choices.

Grammar: Connectors for Cause-Effect Essays

Connectors and **transition words** help show the relationship between a cause and an effect. Study these common cause-effect structures.

Connectors That Show Cause

Simple sentence: introducing a prepositional phrase
As a result of   n   s   v   **Because of**   the rain, we got wet.   **Due to**
Complex sentence: introducing a clause
Because   s   v   s   v   **Since**   it rained, we got wet.

Connectors That Show Effect

BETWEEN SENTENCES	EXAMPLES
It started to rain heavily, and none of us was prepared for it.	**As a result,** we got wet.
	Therefore, we got wet.
	For this reason, we got wet.
	Consequently, we got wet.
	Thus, we got wet.

For a more complete list, see *Connectors* in the *Writer's Handbook*.

A rickshaw in the rain, Kolkata, India

ACTIVITY 5 | Using connectors

Read the essay (focus-on-effects method) and choose the appropriate connector in each set of parentheses.

WORDS TO KNOW Essay 2.4

exposure: (n) an experience of something
impact: (v) to affect
in the long run: (phr) in time; ultimately

intrigued: (adj) fascinated
pose: (v) to present something such as a problem, danger, or difficulty

---

ESSAY 2.4

The Effects of Studying Abroad

1   Globalization[1] has **impacted** all aspects of modern-day life, from a country's commerce and politics to a family's everyday decision making at the grocery store. One element of globalization that is of particular interest in the field of education is study abroad programs. Host countries and institutions are eager to accept international students while the students are **intrigued** by the possibility of international travel. Studying abroad has become an opportunity that is available to many students, especially those at the university level. Certainly, studying abroad is not for everyone [1] (due to / as a result) the challenges it **poses**; however, for those students willing to accept these challenges, the positive effects will stay with them forever.

Studying abroad can have positive long-term effects.

2   One important effect of studying abroad is a student's greater understanding of a different educational system. The curriculum, availability, and types of lectures, and the educational environment as a whole, will likely differ from those of the student's home country. At first the student may be confused, but the **exposure** to a different curriculum will broaden his or her educational horizons **in the long run**. [2] (For this reason / As a result of) the new academic culture, the student will be able to better appreciate his or her own educational setting later after returning home.

3   An individual who studies abroad also develops an understanding of a different culture. Even if the host country's language is the same, the student will have many new cultural experiences. From learning how to live with a host family[2] to trying new foods and customs, the student will come across unfamiliar and sometimes frustrating customs. [3] (Since / Consequently), he or she will need to adapt to rules and behaviors that are unfamiliar. Dinner table customs, the greeting of new people, and gift giving are perfect examples of social behaviors that differ depending on the culture. Leaving behind a comfortable, well-known lifestyle to put himself or herself in an unfamiliar situation challenges the student in ways that can lead to tremendous growth and independence. This life exercise may be difficult in the beginning of the study abroad period, but it becomes easier as time passes and the student develops a better understanding of the host country.

4   Finally, studying abroad gives students the opportunity to serve as ambassadors[3] for their home countries. A foreign student on a university campus can be an uncommon sight. The host institution, including the local student body[4], will form an impression of the student's culture based on interactions with him or her. [4] (As a result / Due to), the student will learn to represent his or her country and culture in the best possible light.

5   To summarize, there are a number of effects of studying abroad, not only for the student but also for the host institution. While some of the experiences may seem difficult at the time, the long-term effects are generally positive. This is in large part [5] (because of / because) globalization in education.

[1]globalization: social and economic interaction between countries
[2]host family: family that takes a foreign student into their home
[3]ambassador: a representative
[4]student body: student population at a particular school

Grammar: Noun Clauses

Noun clauses are dependent clauses. They take the place of a noun or a noun phrase. They can be the subject or object of the main verb, the object of a preposition, or a subject complement.

FUNCTION	NOUN PHRASE	NOUN CLAUSE
subject of main verb	**The pizza** was delicious.	**What I ate for dinner** was delicious.
object of main verb	I don't know **the location of the class.**	I don't know **where the class is.**
object of preposition	The professor is not interested in **the reasons for Paul's absence.**	The professor is not interested in **why Paul is absent.**
subject complement	The main problem is **a lack of workers.**	The main problem is **that there are not enough workers.**

Noun clauses often begin with a question word (*what, when, where, why, who, whom, which, whose,* and *how*). Notice that a noun clause uses statement word order, not question word order.

$$s \quad + \quad v$$

✓ He does not know <u>when the plane will arrive</u>.

✗ He does not know when will the plane arrive.

That can also introduce a noun clause, but it is often omitted:

The main problem is **(that) there are not enough workers.**

ACTIVITY 6 | Scrambled sentences with noun clauses

Unscramble the words and phrases to write complete sentences. Underline the noun clauses.

1. the students / the professor asked / to take the final exam / when they wanted

_____

2. when the new CEO / will be chosen / none of the employees knows

_____

3. that there are / of an engineering degree is / jobs available / one benefit

_____

4. is a mystery / learn foreign languages / while others cannot / can easily / how some people

_____

5. not everyone / that the strategic plan / will work / is convinced

_____

ACTIVITY 7 | Writing noun clauses

Rewrite each sentence using a noun clause.

1. His greatest accomplishment is his climb up Mount Everest.

   His greatest accomplishment is that he climbed Mount Everest.

2. Does anyone know the date for the final exam?

3. No one was interested in the speaker's remarks.

4. The meal we had last night was disappointing.

5. She is still deciding on a topic for the project.

6. Hotel management is a career with growth potential.

Wordiness

Unnecessary words and phrases do not improve your writing. Instead, they make it hard to understand what you want to say. Good writers use the fewest words possible to make a point. In other words, they are **concise**. Study the list of common **wordy** phrases and the equivalent more **concise** phrases.

WORDY	CONCISE
at that point in time	at that time
despite the fact that + subject + verb	despite + noun
for the purpose of	for
in my opinion, I believe . . .	in my opinion . . . *or* I believe . . .
in the event that	if
in the final analysis	finally
it goes without saying that	Ø—use nothing
made a statement saying	said
the reason why is	because
when all is said and done	Ø—use nothing

ACTIVITY 8 | Avoiding wordiness

This introductory paragraph is from a cause-effect essay. It contains five wordy phrases. Underline them. Then, on a separate piece of paper, rewrite the paragraph to make it more concise. Note: You will need to change some words. There is more than one correct way of rewriting this paragraph.

PARAGRAPH 2.1

Fat-Free Food

In my opinion, I believe that the fat-free food industry is a tremendous money-making business. In fact, recent research has shown that fat-free products are considered only a minor prescription for the purpose of losing weight. Nutritionists have made statements saying that the most important steps to losing weight are exercising and eating well-balanced meals. Despite the fact that this information has appeared, many people still seem to believe that, when all is said and done, eating fat-free food is the best dieting method. There are some interesting reasons for this fat-free phenomenon.

Redundancy

Redundancy is the unnecessary repetition of information. You may want to impress your readers with a well-written essay that is full of thought-provoking information. You may think, "The more information I have in my essay, the more my readers will enjoy it." This is not usually the case, especially if, instead of adding information, you repeat what you have already said.

The list contains commonly used **redundant phrases** and the better, more **concise** wording. (If you are not sure why they are redundant, look up the meanings of the two words.)

REDUNDANT	CONCISE
collaborate together	collaborate
completely unanimous	unanimous
courthouse building	courthouse
descend downward	descend
erupt violently	erupt
exactly identical	identical
free gift	gift
loud explosion	explosion
merge together	merge
repeat again	repeat
unexpected surprise	surprise

Notice the redundancy of the underlined information and the more concise sentence.

Redundant: <u>The United States is one of the most influential powers in the world.</u> Partly because of its abundant material resources and political system, <u>the country has great influence in global affairs.</u>

Concise: The United States has great influence in global affairs in part because of its abundant material resources and political system.

ACTIVITY 9 | Don't say it twice

Underline the seven examples of redundant phrases in this paragraph. Then compare your answers with a partner's.

PARAGRAPH 2.2

Out of This World

Many people love to watch science-fiction stories on TV or at the movies. TV shows, movies, and films—such as *Star Trek*—are popular not only because they creatively show how future life might be in 300 years, but also because they introduce us to characters from other worlds, planets, and galaxies. These characters often look very different from humans, which makes them an unexpected surprise. Perhaps one of the most popular kinds of characters in these futuristic programs is a person with superhuman powers. These powers could be physical strength or extreme intelligence. Often these superhumans collaborate together with regular people to defeat an evil force. One must remember, however, that these scenes take place in an untrue and fictitious situation. An interesting idea to think about is what would happen if ordinary, everyday people possessed superhuman powers.

Visitors attend the Middle East Film & Comic Con in Dubai, United Arab Emirates.

BUILDING BETTER VOCABULARY

WORDS TO KNOW

compelling (adj)	fatigued (adj) **AW**	irresponsible (adj)
consequence (n) **AW**	have a point (v phr)	maintain (v) **AW**
correlation (n) **AW**	impact (v) **AW**	motive (n) **AW**
currently (adv)	imply (v) **AW**	pose (v) **AW**
distinguish (v)	inappropriate (adj) **AW**	somewhat (adv) **AW**
exemplify (v)	in the long run (phr)	substantial (adj)
exposure (n) **AW**	in the meantime (phr)	thrive (v)
familiarize (v)	intrigued (adj)	undergo (v) **AW**

ACTIVITY 10 | Word associations

Circle the word or phrase that is more closely related to the bold word or phrase on the left.

1. aspect	addition	feature
2. consequence	cause	result
3. currently	in the future	now
4. exemplify	illustrate	throw out
5. have a point	important	unnecessary
6. intrigued	bored	interested
7. motive	result	reason
8. somewhat	a little	a lot
9. substantial	a little	a lot
10. undergo	discover	transformation

ACTIVITY 11 | Collocations

Fill in the blank with the word that most naturally completes the phrase.

correlation	familiarize	maintain	pose	similar

1. _____ oneself with the material

2. a direct _____

3. _____ a positive attitude

4. a _____ amount of evidence

5. _____ a question

| compelling | distinquish | fatigued | inappropriate | thrive |

6. _____ _____ behavior

7. continue to _____

8. to become physically or mentally _____

9. unable to _____ between

10. a/an _____ reason

ACTIVITY 12 | Word forms

Complete each sentence with the correct word form. Use the correct form of the verbs.

NOUN	VERB	ADJECTIVE	ADVERB	SENTENCES
consequence		consequential	consequentially	**1.** There was a large supply, and _____ the price fell. **2.** The _____ of his bad decision was that he lost his license.
correlation	correlate			**3.** The scientists must be able to _____ their hypothesis to their lab results. **4.** There is a _____ between insomnia and heart health.
current		current	currently	**5.** She is _____ serving as the team leader. **6.** The _____ temperature is higher than normal.
impact	impact	impacted		**7.** After the accident, her views of small cars were negatively _____. **8.** The crater's _____ in the desert can be seen from space.
maintenance	maintain	maintained		**9.** Even though he is extremely fit, he cannot _____ his speed for more than five minutes. **10.** The printer is not too expensive, but the cost of its _____ is quite high.

ACTIVITY 13 | Vocabulary in writing

Choose five words from Words to Know. Write a complete sentence with each word.

1. _____

2. _____

3. _____

4. _____

5. _____

BUILDING BETTER SENTENCES

ACTIVITY 14 | Scrambled sentences

Unscramble the words and phrases to write complete sentences.

1. until next week / as a result / the game was postponed / of the rain,

   _____

   _____

2. he knows the content well / for twenty years, / because he has taught the class

   _____

   _____

3. that the company's / could rise / stock / so suddenly / no one was aware

   _____

   _____

4. her art skills / where she had learned / wanted to know / her classmates

   _____

   _____

5. it is not surprising / engineering field / are going into / the biomedical / that so many students

   _____

   _____

ACTIVITY 15 | Combining sentences

Combine the ideas into one sentence. You may change the word forms, but do not change or omit any ideas. There may be more than one answer. See Unit 1 for more information.

1. There were rumors.
The rumors were mean and untrue.
The rumors were about the new vice president.

_____

_____

2. The graduation was postponed.
The graduation was of a high school.
The weather was bad.
The high school was local.

_____

_____

3. The entrance is closed.
It is the main entrance.
The entrance is to the stadium.
The closure is between 6:00 p.m. and midnight.

_____

_____

ACTIVITY 16 | Describing a scene

On a separate piece of paper, write three or four sentences about the photo. Focus on the causes and the effects of the scene. Make sure that you use at least two noun clauses in your sentences.

WRITING

Steps to Writing an Essay

Many writers can think of good topics, but they have trouble developing their topics into essays. One brainstorming method that helps is to ask questions about the topic. This process often leads to new ideas that can be used in an essay. Especially for a cause-effect essay, good writers ask the question *Why?*

ACTIVITY 17 | Starting with questions

The following questions can all be developed into cause-effect essays. Try to give at least two answers to each question.

1. Why do people post private information?

_____

_____

2. What are the reasons people choose a job or career?

_____

_____

3. Why are more and more people studying a second (or third) language?

_____

_____

4. What are the effects of playing a team sport?

_____

_____

5. What are the causes of _____? (Think of your own topic.)

_____

_____

6. What are the effects of _____? (Think of your own topic.)

_____

_____

ACTIVITY 18 | Brainstorming

Study the following brainstorming technique called **clustering**. In this example, the topic is the effects of ozone depletion on the environment. Then, choose a topic from Activity 17. On a separate piece of paper, brainstorm some ideas about your topic using the clustering method. When you have finished, cross out the ideas that you do not want to include in your essay. Explain your brainstorming cluster to a classmate.

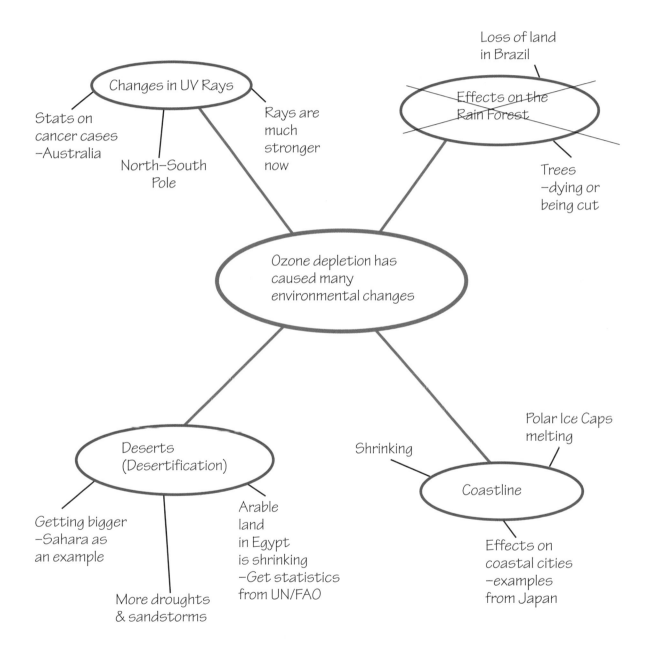

ACTIVITY 19 | Planning with an outline

Complete this outline to help you create a more detailed plan for your cause-effect essay. Use your ideas from Activity 18. You may need more or fewer points under each heading.

Topic:_____

I. Introduction (Paragraph 1)

   A. Hook: _____

   B. Connecting information: _____

        _____

   C. Thesis statement: _____

        _____

II. Body

   A. Paragraph 2 (first cause or effect) topic sentence: _____

        _____

        SUPPORT   **1.** _____

                          2. _____

                          3. _____

   B. Paragraph 3 (second cause or effect) topic sentence: _____

        _____

        SUPPORT   **1.** _____

                          2. _____

                          3. _____

   C. Paragraph 4 (third cause or effect) topic sentence: _____

        _____

        SUPPORT   **1.** _____

                          2. _____

                          3. _____

III. Conclusion (Paragraph 5)

    A. Restated thesis: _____

    _____

    B. Suggestion, prediction, question, or opinion: _____

    _____

WRITER'S NOTE Personal Writing Style

Some writers work well from a detailed outline, and some can write well from a general outline. Some writers write the introduction first, and some write it last. Writing is an individual activity. Use the guidelines in this book and follow the process that works best for you.

ACTIVITY 20 | Peer editing your outline

Exchange books with a partner and look at Activity 19. Read your partner's outline. Then use the Peer Editing Form for Outlines in the *Writer's Handbook* to help you comment on your partner's work. Use your partner's feedback to revise your outline. Make sure you have enough information to develop your supporting sentences.

ACTIVITY 21 | Writing a cause-effect essay

Write a cause-effect essay based on your revised outline from Activity 20. Use at least two of the vocabulary words or phrases presented in the unit. Underline these words and phrases in your essay. If you need ideas for phrasing, see *Useful Words and Phrases* in the *Writer's Handbook*.

Years of erosion by the Colorado River caused the uniquely shaped Horseshoe Bend in the Grand Canyon, Arizona, USA

Peer Editing

Good writers **proofread** their work and rewrite it several times. Think of the first draft of an essay as a first attempt.

Before you rewrite your essay or paper, it is helpful to let someone else read it, offer comments, and ask questions to clarify your meaning. In class, **peer editing** is an easy way to get opinions about your paper. Other students (your peers) read your paper and make comments using a set of questions and guidelines. Peer editing can help you strengthen any areas in your writing that are weak or that appear confusing to the reader.

Here are some suggestions for peer editing:

1. **Listen carefully.** In peer editing, you will receive comments and suggestions from other students. It is important to listen carefully to comments about your writing. You may think that what you wrote is clear and accurate, but readers can often tell you what needs improvement. Remember that the comments are about the writing, not about you.

2. **Make helpful comments.** When you read your classmates' papers, choose your words and comments carefully. Use polite language. For example, instead of saying "This is bad grammar," or "I can't understand any of your ideas," make helpful comments, such as "You need to make sure that every sentence has a verb," or "What do you mean in this sentence?"

3. **Study an example of "Editing Your Writing."** Study *Editing Your Writing* in the *Writer's Handbook*. There are examples of edits and comments that a teacher made on a student's first draft and an example of the student's second draft.

4. **Read, read, read!** It is important for you to understand why a piece of writing is good or is not good, and the best way to do this is to read, read, and read some more. The more writing styles you become familiar with, the better your writing can become, too.

ACTIVITY 22 | Peer editing your essay

Exchange papers from Activity 21 with a partner. Read your partner's essay. Then use Peer Editing Form 2 in the *Writer's Handbook* to help you comment on your partner's writing. Consider your partner's comments as you revise your essay.

Additional Topics for Writing

Here are five ideas for writing a cause-effect essay. Follow your teacher's instructions and choose one or more topics to write about.

TOPIC 1: Look at the photo on pages 38–39 and reread your freewrite. Write an essay on another natural cause-effect relationship, or on a cause-effect relationship between humans and nature, such as pollution and global warming.

TOPIC 2: Young people are experts at using social media, even in school. What are some of the positive effects of using social media in the classroom?

TOPIC 3: Friendships are an integral part of a person's life. Unfortunately, some of these relationships do not last. Write an essay highlighting some of the reasons that friendships sometimes die.

TOPIC 4: Many people enjoy traveling and experiencing other cultures. What are some of the beneficial effects of international travel on an individual?

TOPIC 5: In recent years, car manufacturers have been working to develop automobiles that run on alternative energies. These include solar-powered cars and electric cars. What are some of the effects that this technology will have on society?

TEST PREP

You should spend about 40 minutes on this task. Write a five-paragraph cause-effect essay about the following topic:

Why do people move from one country to another?

Use the focus-on-causes method. Include a short introduction (with a thesis statement), three body paragraphs, and a conclusion.

TIP

Give yourself a few minutes before the end of the task to review your work. Check for spelling, verb tense, and subject-verb agreement mistakes.

---

3 | Comparison Essays

An American cruise ship docks in Havana Bay, Cuba.

OBJECTIVES
- Write a comparison essay
- Use connectors to show comparison and contrast
- Use adjective clauses correctly in an essay

ELEMENTS OF GREAT WRITING

What Is a Comparison Essay?

In a **comparison essay**, you can compare ideas, people, different times in history—any two items that are related in some way. You can focus on the similarities between the two items, on the differences, or on both the similarities and the differences. Your goal is to show—in a meaningful way—how these items are similar or different, what their strengths and weaknesses are, or what their advantages and disadvantages are. In a history class, your essay might compare heroes of the French Revolution and the American Revolution. In an economics class, you might write about the differences between supply-side and demand-side economics. In a computer science class, you might write about the differences between cloud hosting and traditional hosting of data.

Like other essays, the comparison essay has an introductory paragraph that contains a hook and a thesis statement, two or three or more paragraphs that make up the body, and a concluding paragraph.

> **WRITER'S NOTE** Avoiding Common Comparisons
> Good comparison essays do not state the obvious. They show similarities in things that are considered different and, conversely, focus on the differences between things that are considered to be similar.

Re-enactors in uniforms from the American Revolution join a fourth of July parade in Massachusetts, USA.

Patterns of Organization

There are two basic ways to organize a comparison essay—the block method and the point-by-point method.

BLOCK METHOD	POINT-BY-POINT METHOD
Present one subject and all its points of comparison. Then do the same for the second subject. Discuss each subject completely without interruption.	Include both subjects in one point of comparison before moving on to the next point of comparison.

Paragraph 1: Introduction
Thesis: There are two solid options for data storage, each with pros and cons.
 	
Paragraph 2: Cloud data storage
   cost
   ease of use,
   reliability
 	
Paragraph 3: Traditional data storage
   cost
   ease of use,
   reliability
 	
Paragraph 4: Conclusion
	Paragraph 1: Introduction
	Thesis: There are two solid options for data storage, each with pros and cons.
	
	Paragraph 2: Cost
	   cloud data storage
	   traditional data storage
	
	Paragraph 3: Ease of use
	   cloud data storage
	   traditional data storage
	
	Paragraph 4: Reliability
	   cloud data storage
	   traditional data storage
	
	Paragraph 5: Conclusion

No matter which method of organization you choose, the information in a comparison essay must be presented in the same order. In the block-method example, notice that in Paragraph 2, all the important information about cloud data storage is presented (cost, ease of use, and reliability). The supporting information in Paragraph 3 also includes these three aspects in the same order with the focus on traditional data storage.

In the point-by-point method, the points of development are also cost, ease of use, and reliability. Each paragraph contains information about both storage systems.

ACTIVITY 1 | Comparing methods of organization

Review the two methods of organizing a comparison essay. Consider the advantages and disadvantages of both. Work with a partner to answer the questions.

1. Which method, block or point-by-point, requires more paragraphs?

2. Which is likely easier to organize and write?

3. As a reader, in which method are the points of comparison easier to follow?

ACTIVITY 2 | Analyzing a comparison essay

This essay compares some features of Brazil and the United States. Discuss the questions below. Then read the comparison essay and answer the questions that follow.

1. How many different countries have you visited? Which of these countries felt "comfortable" to you? Which countries were very different from your own?

2. What does the word *individualism* mean to you?

WORDS TO KNOW Essay 3.1

asset: (n) an advantage
core: (n) center, essential part
disruptive: (adj) troublesome, disorderly
diversity: (n) variety
ethnic: (adj) sharing cultural characteristics

focus on: (v) to concentrate on
massive: (adj) huge
remarkable: (adj) amazing, extraordinary
unique: (adj) one of a kind, distinctive

ESSAY 3.1

Not as Different as One Would Think

1 All countries are **unique**. Obviously, countries are different from one another in location, size, language, government, climate, and lifestyle. Some countries, however, share some surprising similarities. In this case, Brazil and the United States come to mind. Some may think that these two nations have very little in common because they are in different hemispheres[1]. On the contrary, the two countries share many similarities.

2   One important similarity between Brazil and the United States is their **massive** size. Both Brazil and the United States are extremely large countries. Brazil covers almost half of the South American continent. It has a land mass of nearly 3.3 million square miles (8.5 million square kilometers) and is home to cosmopolitan[2] centers such as Rio de Janeiro and São Paulo. Due to its size, few Brazilians can say that they have traveled extensively within the country's borders. Like Brazil, the United States takes up a significant portion of its continent (North America). It extends from the Atlantic Ocean to the Pacific Ocean and has a land mass of 3.1 million square miles (8 million square kilometers), not including Alaska, Hawaii, and other territories. It is home to world-famous cities such as Los Angeles and New York. As a result of its size, it is fair to say that many people in the United States have not visited much of their country.

3   Another similarity between Brazil and the United States is the **diversity** of the population. Brazil was colonized[3] by Europeans, and its culture has been greatly influenced by this fact. However, Brazilians' identity was influenced by many other cultures as well. Brazil is a "melting pot" of many **ethnic** groups that immigrated there and mixed with the indigenous[4] people. The United States also has a diversity of ethnic groups, from the Native American population and early colonists from northern Europe to slave groups from Africa. Later immigrants from the Mediterranean, Asia, and South America added to the diversity of its citizens. The mixture of cultures and customs has worked to form ethnically rich cultures in both countries.

4   Finally, both countries share an important value: individualism. Brazil works hard to defend the concept of freedom of choice. Citizens believe that they have the right to do and be whatever they desire as long as they do not hurt others. This attitude was introduced in the 1930s and 1940s by Brazilian President Getúlio Vargas. He was responsible for establishing an individualistic government that helped modernize and industrialize the country. Individualism is also at the **core** of the culture in the United States, dating back to the Declaration of Independence and the Bill of Rights. Both documents **focus on** individuals' many rights. Some people may believe that the desire for individual expression is **disruptive** and can make a country weak. However, the ability of people to be whatever they want is an **asset** to both countries.

5   Although Brazil and the United States have many differences, they also have **remarkable** similarities in their size, ethnic diversity, and core values. Some people believe that their culture and country are without equal. However, as with these two countries, a closer inspection shows that cultures everywhere have more in common than not.

[1]hemisphere: half of the earth
[2]cosmopolitan: international
[3]colonized: settled
[4]indigenous: native; original

1. What is the main purpose of this essay? Begin with *The purpose is...*

_____

2. Which three things (points of development) about Brazil and the United States does this essay compare?

_____

_____

3. What method of organization does the writer use—point-by-point or block?

_____

4. What is the hook for this essay? Write it here.

_____

5. Underline the thesis statement. Is the thesis restated in the conclusion? If yes, underline the sentence that restates the thesis.

6. In Paragraph 2, the author describes the size of Brazil and the United States. List the supporting information the writer uses.

_____

_____

_____

7. Reread the concluding paragraph of Essay 3.1. Does the writer offer a suggestion, an opinion, a question, or a prediction?

_____

Rio de Janeiro, Brazil

ACTIVITY 3 │ Understanding the elements of a comparison essay

Below is an outline for essay 3.1. Some of the information is missing. Reread the essay and complete the outline.

Title: _____

I. Introduction (Paragraph 1)

    A. Hook: _____

    B. Connecting information: Different location, size, language, government, climate, lifestyle

    C. Thesis statement: _____

    _____

II. Body

    A. Paragraph 2 (Similarity 1) topic sentence: _____

    _____

        1. Brazil's characteristics

            a. Size: _____

            b. Travel: Few Brazilians have traveled extensively in their country.

        2. _____

            a. Size: covers most of North America, extends from Atlantic to Pacific Oceans, 3.1 million square miles (8 million square kilometers)

            b. Travel: _____

            _____

SUPPORT

    B. Paragraph 3 (Similarity 2) topic sentence: Another similarity between Brazil and the United States is the diversity of the population.

        1. Brazil

            a. _____

            b. Other ethnic groups

            c. _____

SUPPORT

2. United States

    a. Native Americans

    b. Northern Europe

    c. _____

    d. Later immigrants from Mediterranean

    e. _____

    f. _____

C. Paragraph 4 (Similarity 3) topic sentence: _____

_____

1. Brazilians' belief in freedom: have the right to do and be whatever they want if don't hurt others, from President Getúlio Vargas in 1930s and 40s

2. U.S. belief in freedom: _____

_____

_____

III. Conclusion (Paragraph 5)

A. Restated thesis: _____

_____

_____

B. Opinion: All cultures are more similar than different.

WRITER'S NOTE Asking Questions

One of the best ways to develop details and facts that will support your main ideas (topic sentences) in each body paragraph is to ask yourself questions about the topic—*Where? Why? When? Who? What? How?*

Developing a Comparison Essay: Supporting Information

ACTIVITY 4 | Writing supporting information

Follow these steps.

1. Essay 3.2 includes an introduction, three topic sentences, and a conclusion. Develop each body paragraph with supporting information. You may write on a separate piece of paper.

2. After you finish, compare your supporting information with that of other students. (Note: This essay follows the point-by-point organizational pattern.)

WORDS TO KNOW Essay 3.2

consideration: (n) careful and mindful thought
eliminate: (v) to remove, destroy
intimidate: (v) to persuade by using fear

overwhelming: (adj) emotionally or physically overpowering
purchase: (n) anything that is bought

An ice cave within a glacier in Vatnajokull National Park, Iceland

ESSAY 3.2

Smartphone Choices

1   Some years ago, people were **intimidated** by shopping for a smartphone. For one, smartphone technology was so new that many people were afraid of it. It was also extremely expensive, and many consumers were not sure if these phones would soon be replaced by yet another new technology. History, of course, has shown that smartphones are here to stay.

Not only that, but they are getting smarter and smarter every year. Today's smartphone shoppers need to know what their two main options are. Although the technology is no longer new, it can still be intimidating to shop for a smartphone. Consumers can **eliminate** some of this fear by doing their homework first. One of the biggest **considerations** for a smartphone **purchase** is iOS or Android. To reach a decision, a buyer can compare these two operating systems in terms of their overall cost, convenience, and style.

2   iOS and Android devices can differ in their cost. _____

_____

_____

_____

3   Another thing to consider is the convenience factor, such as the availability of certain apps. _____

_____

_____

_____

4   Finally, there is the subject of style. _____

_____

_____

_____

5   Choosing between these two types of smartphones is a personal decision for the consumer. This decision can be made more easily by looking at cost, convenience, and style preferences. While it can seem like an **overwhelming** task now, it certainly will not get any easier as more and more advanced smartphones come on the market.

Grammar: Connectors for Comparison Essays

Connectors help readers by providing logical connections between sentences, ideas, and paragraphs. Some connectors show comparison between sentences or ideas, and others show contrast or concession. Notice the use of commas with these connectors.

Connectors That Show Comparison between Sentences

COMPARISON	EXAMPLES
In addition, subject + verb.	Both Red Beauty and Midnight Dream roses are known for the size of their blooms, their color, and their fragrance. **In addition,** they are easy to grow.
Similarly, subject + verb.	The Midnight Dream rose won awards in local contests last year. **Similarly,** the Red Beauty rose was singled out for its beauty.
Likewise, subject + verb.	The blooms of Red Beauty roses last longer than those of most other roses. **Likewise,** the blooms of the Midnight Dream rose are long lasting.
Compared to subject, + verb.	Some roses last for a very short time. **Compared to** these roses, the blooms of Red Beauty and Midnight Dream roses last a long time.

Connectors That Show Contrast or Concession between Sentences

CONTRAST OR CONCESSION	EXAMPLES
However, subject + verb. *or* **Nevertheless,** subject + verb.	Many differences are clear to even beginner gardeners. **Nevertheless,** some of their differences are not very obvious.
On the other hand, subject + verb.	Some people find gardening dull. **On the other hand,** some people like nothing better than to work in their gardens.
In contrast, subject + verb.	Red Beauty has a strong, sweet fragrance. **In contrast,** Midnight Dream's fragrance is light and fruity.
Although subject + verb, subject + verb.	Both Midnight Dream roses and Red Beauty roses are red. **Although** both varieties produce red flowers, Midnight Dream roses are much darker than Red Beauty roses.
Even though subject + verb, subject + verb.	Red Beauty roses and Midnight Dream roses are long-stemmed. **Even though** both of these species are long stemmed, Red Beauty stems are thinner and covered with thorns.
Unlike noun, subject + verb.	What do we know about the cost of these two kinds of roses? **Unlike** Red Beauty, Midnight Dream roses are relatively inexpensive.

ACTIVITY 5 | Using connectors

Read the essay and choose the appropriate connectors. Refer to the grammar charts if necessary.

> **WORDS TO KNOW** Essay 3.3
>
> **harm:** (n) damage or injury
> **in essence:** (phr) basically
> **lenient:** (adj) tolerant, compassionate
> **monitor:** (v) to observe something attentively
>
> **pretend:** (v) to imagine, act as if something were true
> **scenario:** (n) a situation, circumstance
> **when it comes to:** (phr) with regards to

ESSAY 3.3

Parenting 101

1   The film previews are finished, and the movie theater is quiet as everyone waits for the feature film to begin. [1](However / In contrast), the stillness is suddenly broken by a noise. The audience hears a sniffle[1]. The sniffle soon turns to a cry, then a wail. There is an uncomfortable, or perhaps unhappy, toddler sitting in the movie theater. People start shuffling in their seats as they wait for what will happen next. Will the child be taken out of the theater, or will the parent **pretend** that everything is OK? **Scenarios** like these happen regularly. The parents' reaction depends on their parenting style. The two extremes are the **lenient** (laissez-faire[2]) parent and the strict disciplinarian[3] parent.

2   Lenient parents often focus on their child having fun and enjoying being a kid. If a child does something careless like break a glass, lenient parents will not become angry or scream. They know that the child is probably experimenting and meant no **harm**. Likewise, the parents may even explain to the child that it was an accident and the child should not be upset. [2](In contrast / Similarly), lenient parents may not be too concerned about following a schedule. They will allow their children to stay up late and experience new things. The motto "You're only a kid once!" rings very true to these free spirits. These types of parents see themselves as guides for their children, which cannot be said about the second parenting group: the disciplinarians.

Every parent has a different style. This father encourages his children to play and joins them in having fun.

3   Disciplinarian parents consider themselves role models for their children. [3](Unlike / Similarly) lenient parents, their main priorities are the safety and protection of their children. **In essence**, children are **monitored** very carefully and may not be allowed to play outside, interact with animals, or roughhouse[4] in general. A child who experiences a strict upbringing may be encouraged to focus on his or her studies instead of making friends. [4](In addition / However), interaction may be limited to only close family members. Children who are raised in highly disciplined environments are typically very focused on their schoolwork.

4   In the end, no parents are truly 100 percent lenient or 100 percent strict **when it comes to** raising their child. Most fall somewhere in the middle depending on the child, the environment, and the particular situation. [5](Nevertheless / Similarly), parents clearly lean toward one or the other parenting style. Society knows that both child-rearing styles have advantages and disadvantages, but the more interesting question is this: Which style will these children choose when the time comes for them to become parents?

[1]sniffle: a breath taken in through the nose
[2]laissez-faire: French for *not interfering*; "leave it alone"
[3]disciplinarian: a person who believes in and demands obedience to rules
[4]roughhouse: to play in a rough way

Grammar: Subject Adjective Clauses

An adjective clause (also called a relative clause) is a group of words that describes or identifies the noun or pronoun that comes before it. An adjective clause must have a subject and a verb. In a subject adjective clause, the relative pronoun (*that, which,* or *who*) is the subject of the clause. Study the following rules and examples:

EXPLANATION	EXAMPLE
Use *that* or *which* for things.	adjective clause S V The textbook that is required for the class is sold out.
Use *who* or *that* for people.	adjective clause S V The teacher who started the arts program has retired.
If the information in the adjective clause is necessary to clarify the person or thing it describes, do not use a comma to separate the ideas.	adjective clause S V The Florida city that is most popular with tourists is Orlando.
If the information in the adjective clause is not necessary to understand the sentence, use comma(s) to separate the adjective clause. Commas indicate the information is extra. In nonessential clauses, do not use the pronoun *that*.	adjective clause S V Orlando, which is located in Florida, is popular with tourists.

Adjective clauses are a way to combine two ideas (simple sentences) into one complex sentence. Study the following examples:

SIMPLE SENTENCES	COMPLEX SENTENCES WITH ADJECTIVE CLAUSES
The shop is always very busy. The shop sells used sports cars.	The shop **that sells used sports cars** is always very busy.
Samir studies at a university. The university is well known for its technology programs.	Samir studies at a university **that is well known for its technology programs.**
The Khan Academy is a free online tutoring service. It focuses on science and technology education.	The Khan Academy, **which focuses on science and technology education**, is a free online tutoring service.

ACTIVITY 6 | Writing adjective clauses

Read the following introduction to a comparison essay on vacations. Use the information in parentheses to write adjective clauses. Write the new sentences with adjective clauses on a separate piece of paper.

WORDS TO KNOW Essay 3.4

affordable: (adj) inexpensive
burden: (n) a worrying responsibility

integral: (adj) essential, necessary
numerous: (adj) many

ESSAY 3.4

The Benefits of Taking Vacation

(Vacations are an **integral** part of life. Vacations can range from a few days to months.)[1] _Vacations, which can range from a few days to months, are an integral part of life_ . Taking time off from school or work has **numerous** benefits on the mind, body, and spirit. (Some people might have to spend a lot of money. These people wait too long.)[2] _____. However, the news is not all bad. There are some **affordable** vacation options. For instance, some people might prefer to stay home. (A "staycation" is a good alternative. A staycation involves relaxing at home without the **burden** of school or work.)[3] _____. Time off regenerates the individual and cannot be undervalued. Regardless of the destination, whether a traditional vacation or a staycation, (time off is necessary for everyone. The time off should be relaxing.)[4] _____.

ACTIVITY 7 | Writing more adjective clauses

Complete each sentence with an adjective clause.

1. The employee wants a supervisor who _____.

2. World War II was an unforgettable event in history that _____.

3. The town government passed a law that _____.

4. The animals that _____ are in danger of becoming extinct.

5. The Eiffel Tower, which _____, is located in Paris.

BUILDING BETTER VOCABULARY

WORDS TO KNOW

affordable (adj)	focus on (v) `AW`	numerous (adj)
asset (n)	harm (n)	overwhelming (adj)
burden (n)	in essence (phr) `AW`	pretend (v)
consideration (n)	integral (adj) `AW`	purchase (n) `AW`
core (n) `AW`	intimidate (v)	remarkable (adj)
disruptive (adj)	lenient (adj)	scenario (n) `AW`
diversity (n) `AW`	massive (adj)	unique (adj) `AW`
eliminate (v) `AW`	monitor (v) `AW`	when it comes to (phr)
ethnic (adj) `AW`		

ACTIVITY 8 | Word associations

Circle the word or phrase that is more closely related to the bold word or phrase on the left.

1. **affordable**   expensive   inexpensive

2. **asset**   useless   valuable

3. **burden**   difficult   easy

4. **eliminate**   get rid of   keep

5. **ethnic**   water   food

6. **in essence**   basically   uniquely

7. **integral**   important   lucky

8. **monitor**   keep   watch

9. **pretend**   imagine   understand

10. **unique**   many   one

ACTIVITY 9 | Collocations

Fill in the blank with the word or phrase that most naturally completes the phrase.

| core | lenient | numerous | remarkable | scenario |

1. best-case _____

2. _____ approach to parenting

3. _____ complaints

4. a _____ recovery

5. _____ values

| consideration | disruptive | diversity | focus on | massive |

6. _____ the positive

7. _____ of opinions

8. _____ behavior

9. careful _____

10. _____ explosion

ACTIVITY 10 | Word forms

Complete each sentence with the correct word form. Use the correct form of the verbs.

NOUN	VERB	ADJECTIVE	ADVERB	SENTENCES
diversity	diversify	diverse	diversely	1. The _____ types of palm trees found in the Middle East are fascinating. 2. One of the most interesting aspects of the Moonwalker Corporation is the _____ of its employees.
harm	harm	harmful	harmfully	3. Doctors take an oath to do no _____ to their patients. 4. It is widely known that cigarettes are _____ to one's health.

NOUN	VERB	ADJECTIVE	ADVERB	SENTENCES
intimidation	intimidate	intimidated / intimidating		5. The lawyer ——————— the witness during the trial. 6. ——————— is what bullies use to frighten their victims.
remark	remark	**remarkable**	remarkably	7. ———————, the premature baby survived the operation. 8. It was a ——————— movie; it is no wonder it won an Academy Award.
uniqueness		**unique**	uniquely	9. Her ——————— skill of foreseeing problems has helped her advance in her career. 10. The ——————— of sharks compared to other animals interests scientists.

ACTIVITY 11 | Vocabulary in writing

Choose five words from Words to Know. Write a complete sentence with each word.

1. _____

2. _____

3. _____

4. _____

5. _____

Great white sharks are warm-blooded fish, one of the many traits that make them unique.

BUILDING BETTER SENTENCES

ACTIVITY 12 | Writing about photos

On a separate piece of paper, write three to five sentences comparing and contrasting the two photos.

ACTIVITY 13 | Combining sentences

Combine the ideas into one sentence. You may change the word forms, but do not change or omit any ideas. There may be more than one answer.

1. The city of Pompeii had plumbing.

    The plumbing was extremely modern.

    The city was destroyed by a volcanic eruption.

    The eruption happened in AD 79.

    _____

    _____

2. The adult human body has bones.

    There are 206 bones in the adult human body.

    A baby's body has 270 bones.

    Two-hundred and seventy is an approximate number.

    _____

    _____

3. The highest temperature on Earth was in El Azizia, Libya.
The temperature was recorded.
The temperature peaked at 136 degrees Fahrenheit.

_____

_____

ACTIVITY 14 | Scrambled sentences

Unscramble the words and phrases to write complete sentences. Be sure to punctuate correctly.

1. is often crowded / especially on weekends / with the best selection / the bookstore

_____

_____

2. the only metal / at room temperature / Mercury is / that is liquid

_____

_____

3. is Florence / one of the most visited cities / which is home of the Renaissance / in Italy

_____

_____

4. is one of the / of the 21st century / of the driverless car / most fascinating advancements / the development

_____

_____

5. which is also known as the Hijri calendar / the cycles of the moon / the Islamic calendar / is based on

_____

_____

WRITING

Developing Ideas for Writing: Brainstorming

You may be asked to write comparison essays in your classes. Often, you will be given the two subjects to be compared, such as two poems from a literature course, two political beliefs from a political science course, or an invention and a discovery from a history or science course. When you have to choose your subjects for comparison, the following brainstorming tips will help you.

Tips for Brainstorming Topics

1. **The two topics should have something in common.** For example, eating at home and eating out in a restaurant are both examples of places where people can get a meal. Eating at home and going out to see a movie are both activities, but they do not have enough in common to compare easily.

2. **The two topics must also have some differences.** For example, the most obvious differences between eating at home and eating in a restaurant are atmosphere, cost, and food variety. Eating eggs at home and eating pasta at home do not have enough differences to make for an interesting comparison.

3. **You need to have enough information on each topic to make your comparisons.** If you choose two topics that are not well known, it might be more difficult to come up with information. For example, an essay comparing eating at home and eating at your neighbor's home, which you've never visited, would be difficult to support.

Making a List

A good way to determine whether you have enough information about similarities and differences between two topics is to brainstorm a list. Read the information in the lists.

Eating at home	Eating in a restaurant
atmosphere always the same	atmosphere varies depending on restaurant
less expensive	more expensive: paying for food AND service
limited food options—you eat what's been prepared	can choose from a variety of food on the menu
(food can be cooked in different ways)	(food can be cooked in different ways)
(eat with family members)	(eat with family members)

Notice that the similarities are circled. These are "links" between the two subjects. A writer could use these links to highlight the similarities between the two options or to lead into a discussion of the differences between them: "Although food can be cooked in different ways whether eating at home or eating in a restaurant, more people prefer. . ."

Making a Venn Diagram

Another way to brainstorm similarities and differences is to use a Venn diagram. A Venn diagram is a visual representation of the similarities and differences between two concepts. The middle area, where the two circles overlap, shows the similarities. This Venn diagram compares the characteristics of eating at home and eating in a restaurant.

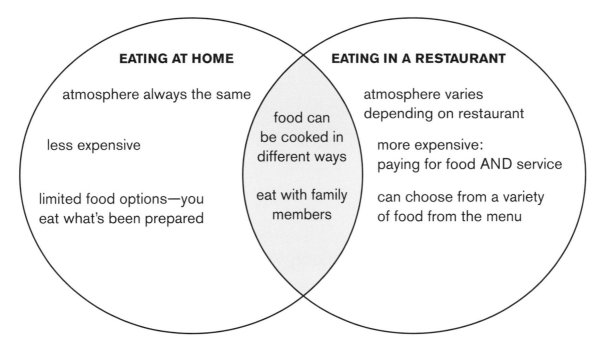

EATING AT HOME

atmosphere always the same

less expensive

limited food options—you eat what's been prepared

food can be cooked in different ways

eat with family members

EATING IN A RESTAURANT

atmosphere varies depending on restaurant

more expensive: paying for food AND service

can choose from a variety of food from the menu

ACTIVITY 15 | Identifying topics for a comparison essay

Below are pairs of potential topics for a comparison essay. Write *yes* under the pairs that would be good and explain briefly what characteristics could be compared. Write *no* under topics that would not be good choices and change one or both of them into more suitable topics.

1. living in a house/living in an apartment

yes—compare costs, privacy, space

2. international travel/domestic travel

3. high school/college

4. the weather in Toronto/tourist attractions in Toronto

5. wild animals/animals in a zoo

6. computers/computer keyboards

_____

7. hands/feet

_____

8. the surface of the ocean floor/the surface of the continents

_____

9. Earth/the North American continent

_____

10. Chinese food/Mexican food

_____

ACTIVITY 16 | Brainstorming: working with a topic

Complete the following steps to develop ideas for a comparison essay.

1. Choose one topic from the list or use your own idea for a topic. If you want to use an original idea, talk to your teacher to see if it is appropriate for a comparison essay.

two movies	two systems of education
two machines	two professions
two famous people	two desserts

2. Review the two brainstorming methods from this unit. Fill in the following chart to brainstorm a list of information about each subject.

TOPIC:	
Subject 1:	**Subject 2:**
_____	_____
_____	_____
_____	_____
_____	_____

3. Now fill in the Venn diagram using the same information you wrote in the chart.

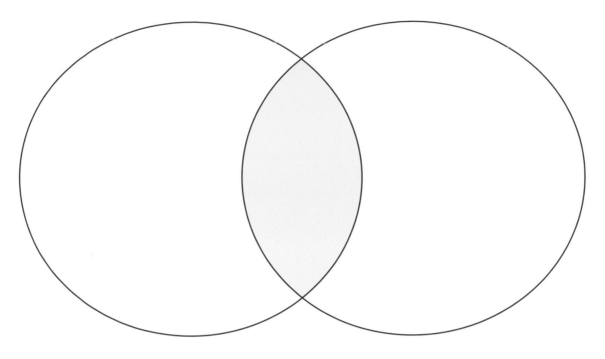

4. Decide if you are going to focus on the similarities or the differences between the two subjects or both in your comparison essay. Then choose three or four main points of comparison that you will use and list them here.

a. _____

b. _____

c. _____

d. _____

Comparing desserts at a cake shop in Melbourne, Australia

ACTIVITY 17 | Creating an outline

Use the following outline to help you brainstorm a more detailed plan for your comparison essay. For this activity, use the point-by-point method of organization. Remember that the point-by-point method organizes each paragraph by one point of development. Include your ideas from Activity 16.

Topic: _____

I. Introduction (Paragraph 1)

    A. Hook: _____

    _____

    B. Connecting information: _____

    _____

    _____

    C. Thesis statement: _____

    _____

II. Body

    A. Paragraph 2 (first point of comparison) topic sentence: _____

    _____

SUPPORT

      1. _____

        a. _____

        b. _____

      2. _____

        a. _____

        b. _____

B. Paragraph 3 (second point of comparison) topic sentence: _____

_____

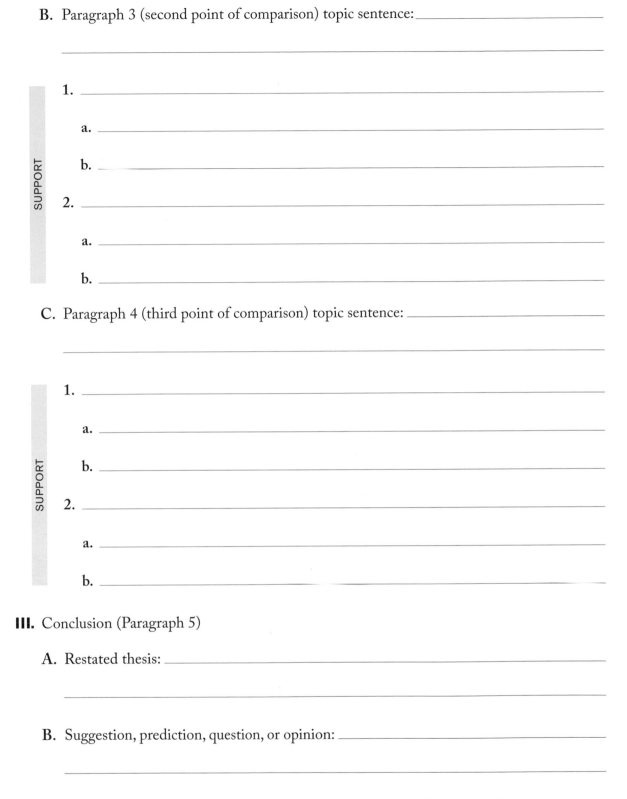

SUPPORT

    1. _____

        a. _____

        b. _____

    2. _____

        a. _____

        b. _____

C. Paragraph 4 (third point of comparison) topic sentence: _____

_____

SUPPORT

    1. _____

        a. _____

        b. _____

    2. _____

        a. _____

        b. _____

III. Conclusion (Paragraph 5)

  A. Restated thesis: _____

_____

  B. Suggestion, prediction, question, or opinion: _____

_____

If you need ideas for phrasing, see *Useful Words and Phrases* in the *Writer's Handbook*.

ACTIVITY 18 | Peer editing your outline

Exchange books with a partner and look at Activity 17. Read your partner's outline. Then use the Peer Editing Form for Outlines in the *Writer's Handbook* to help you comment on your partner's work. Be sure to offer positive suggestions and comments that will help your partner write a better outline and essay. Use your partner's feedback to revise your own outline. Make sure you have enough information to develop your supporting sentences.

ACTIVITY 19 | Writing a comparison essay

Write a comparison essay based on your revised outline from Activity 18. Use at least two of the vocabulary words or phrases presented in the unit. Underline these words and phrases in your essay. Be sure to refer to *Steps in the Writing Process* in the *Writer's Handbook*.

ACTIVITY 20 | Editing your essay

Exchange papers from Activity 19 with a partner. Read your partner's essay. Then use Peer Editing Form 3 in the *Writer's Handbook* to help you comment on your partner's writing. Be sure to offer positive suggestions and comments that will help your partner improve his or her essay. Consider your partner's comments as you revise your essay.

Going camping is more complicated with a baby.

Additional Topics for Writing

Here are five ideas for writing a comparison essay. Follow your teacher's instructions and choose one or more topics to write about.

TOPIC 1: Compare or contrast two places that you have visited. How are these places alike or different? Consider each place's geography, weather, food, language, etc.

TOPIC 2: Compare a couple's life before and after having a baby. What activities are no longer done after having a baby? What activities are more difficult? What are some new experiences that couples have after having a baby?

TOPIC 3: Choose two famous athletes that play the same sport. Write a comparison essay about how they are similar or different. A few points of comparison might be skill, background, and popularity.

TOPIC 4: Explain how long-distance transportation is different today from 100 years ago. How did people travel long distances before modern inventions such as the airplane?

TOPIC 5: Show the similarities and/or differences in the ways that two cultures celebrate an important event, such as a birthday, wedding, or funeral.

TEST PREP

> **TIP**
>
> Make sure that you understand the writing prompt or question. Every timed writing activity is asking for a particular rhetorical style. If the writing topic asks for an explanation, you must explain. If it asks for a comparison, focus on writing a comparison. Do not risk getting points taken off your timed writing because you did not respond to the writing prompt.

You should spend about 40 minutes on this task. Write a comparison essay about the following topic:

Compare two popular vacation destinations.

For this assignment, use the point-by-point method. Remember to double space your essay. Include a short introduction with a thesis statement, three body paragraphs, and a brief conclusion. Write at least 250 words.

---

4 | Argument Essays

An endangered Northern spotted owl, a source of great controversy in logging communities of the Pacific Northwest, rests in a clear-cut area near Merlin, Oregon, USA.

OBJECTIVES
- Write an argument essay
- Control tone with modals
- Avoid faulty logic
- Use *if* clauses correctly in sentences

FREEWRITE | Look at the photo and read the caption. What are your ideas about nature conservation? What is more important: nature or industry, such as logging? Write your ideas on a separate piece of paper.

ELEMENTS OF GREAT WRITING

What Is an Argument Essay?

In an **argument essay**, sometimes referred to as a **persuasive essay**, the writer's purpose is to persuade the audience to agree with his or her ideas about a controversial topic. In a sociology class, for example, you might write an essay arguing that female military personnel can be as effective as male military personnel in combat missions. In a history class, your essay might try to convince readers that World War I could have been avoided if certain steps had been taken. In an argument essay, the writer states the claim or belief, gives reasons to support it, and tries to convince the reader that he or she is correct.

Arguing Pro or Con

Choosing a topic that is appropriate for an argument essay is especially important because some things cannot be argued. For example, you cannot argue that Mexican food is *better* than Indian food because this is a personal opinion that cannot be supported by facts. However, you can argue that Mexican food is *more popular* than Indian food in the United States and support the argument with facts about the number of Mexican restaurants. Similarly, you cannot argue against the statement that jazz music was created by African Americans. It is a statement of fact; therefore, you cannot write an argument essay using this as your thesis statement.

Here are a few topics and suitable thesis statements for an argument essay:

- Driving — Drivers should not be able to perform certain activities while driving, such as eating, talking on a phone, or putting on makeup.

- Standardized testing — Standardized testing should not be required as part of the application process for universities.

- Fast-food restaurants — Fast-food restaurants ought to list the calorie counts for all items on their menus.

You can argue either for (**pro**) or against (**con**) these statements. If your topic does not have two viewpoints, your essay will not be effective.

Convincing the Reader

Your job as the writer of an argument essay is to convince your readers that the idea you are presenting (your thesis statement) is the most valid viewpoint. To do this, your essay needs to be based on logic, not emotion, and it must include an opposing viewpoint, or **counterargument**. Even though you are arguing one side of an issue (either for or against it), you must think about what someone on the other side of the issue would argue. As soon as you give your opponent's point of view, you must offer a **refutation** of it. This means that you refute the other point of view, or show how it is wrong.

ACTIVITY 1 | Analyzing an argument essay

Discuss the questions. Then read the argument essay and answer the questions that follow.

1. Did you wear a uniform when you went to school?

2. Some people believe that children are too materialistic, or concerned with money and possessions, these days. For example, they may be too interested in wearing brand-name clothes and shoes, such as Gucci or Nike. What is your opinion?

WORDS TO KNOW Essay 4.1

associated with: (adj) connected to; related to
implement: (v) to apply; put into practice
incident: (n) an occurrence, happening
merit: (n) value; worth
on the surface: (phr) examined superficially
opponent: (n) someone who disagrees with a person or idea

punishment: (n) a penalty for doing something wrong
unity: (n) a connection among individuals; harmony
wealth: (n) a large amount of money or property; fortune

ESSAY 4.1

The School Uniform Question

1   Individualism is a fundamental part of society in the United States. Most people believe in the right to express themselves without fear of **punishment**. This value, however, is at odds with a recent trend. In the 2013–2014 school year, one in five U.S. public schools required students to wear uniforms, up from one in eight a decade earlier. Should we honor individualism above all else and allow public school students to make decisions about clothing, or should all students be required to wear a uniform? School uniforms are the better choice for three reasons.

2   First, wearing school uniforms would help make students' lives simpler. They would no longer have to decide what to wear every morning, sometimes trying on outfit after outfit in an effort to choose. The time saved from not having to search for a "cool" outfit early in the morning would be significant. Students could spend more time having a proper breakfast or reviewing class notes before going to school rather than staring at a closet full of clothes. Wearing uniforms instead of street clothes would not only save time, but also eliminate the stress often **associated with** this chore.

3   Second, school uniforms influence students to act responsibly in groups and as individuals. Uniforms give students the message that school is a special place for learning. In addition, uniforms create a feeling of **unity** among students. For example, when students do something as a group, such as attend meetings in the auditorium or eat lunch in the cafeteria, the fact that they all wear the same uniform gives them a sense of community. This sense of unity may also reduce the number of negative **incidents** that occur in schools. Students who attend schools that require the wearing of school uniforms actually feel safer than students who do not attend these schools.

4   Finally, school uniforms would help make all students feel equal. Students' standards of living differ greatly from family to family. Some people are well off while others are not. People sometimes forget that school is a place to get an education, not to promote a "fashion show." **Implementing** mandatory school uniforms would make all students look the same regardless of their financial status. School uniforms would promote pride and help to raise the self-esteem of students who cannot afford to wear expensive clothing.

5   **Opponents** of mandatory uniforms say that students who wear school uniforms cannot express their individuality. **On the surface**, this point has some **merit**. However, as stated previously, school is a place to learn, not to show off **wealth** or style. Society must decide if individual expression through clothing is more valuable than encouraging students to focus on what is really important at school: their studies. It is important to remember that school uniforms are worn only during school hours. Students can use fashion to express their individuality outside of the classroom. They can also express their individuality in school in other ways, such as by the activities and clubs in which they choose to participate.

6   In conclusion, there are many well-documented benefits of implementing mandatory school uniforms for students, among them making students' lives simpler, encouraging them to act more responsibly, and making them all feel equal. Public schools should require uniforms in order to benefit both the students and society as a whole.

1. What is the main purpose of this essay? Begin with *The purpose is ...*

_____

_____

2. What is the thesis statement? _____

_____

3. Paragraphs 2, 3, and 4 each give a reason for requiring school uniforms. These reasons can be found in the topic sentence of each paragraph. What are the reasons?

Paragraph 2: _____

Paragraph 3: _____

Paragraph 4: _____

4. In Paragraph 4, what supporting information does the writer give to show that uniforms make students equal?

_____

_____

5. What is the counterargument to the thesis?

_____

_____

6. The writer gives a refutation of the counterargument by showing that it is invalid. What is

the writer's refutation? _____

_____

7. Write the sentence from the concluding paragraph that restates the thesis.

_____

_____

Developing an Argument Essay

ACTIVITY 2 | Outlining an argument essay

The following outline is missing a topic sentence and some supporting information. Work with a partner to complete the outline. Use your knowledge of the topic and understanding of essay organization. After you finish, compare your answers with other students' work.

Topic: Physical education in school

I. Introduction (Paragraph 1)

Thesis statement: Physical education classes should be required for all public school students in all grades.

II. Body

A. Paragraph 2 topic sentence: Physical education courses promote children's general health.

> SUPPORT

   1. Researchers have proved that exercise has maximum benefit if done regularly.

   2. _____

   3. Students should learn the importance of physical fitness at an early age.

B. Paragraph 3 topic sentence: Physical education teaches children transferable life skills.

> SUPPORT

   1. Kids learn about teamwork while playing team sports.

   2. Kids learn about the benefits of healthy competition.

   3. _____

C. Paragraph 4 topic sentence: _____

_____

> SUPPORT

   1. Trained physical education teachers can teach more effectively than parents.

   2. Physical education teachers can point students toward new and interesting sports.

   3. Schools generally have the appropriate facilities and equipment.

D. Paragraph 5 (counterargument and refutation)

SUPPORT

    1. Counterargument: Some parents might disagree and claim that only academic subjects should be taught in school.

    2. Refutation: Then again, most parents do not have the time or the resources to make sure that their children are getting enough exercise.

III.   Conclusion (Paragraph 6) (restated thesis):

_____

_____

ACTIVITY 3 | Writing supporting information

In this essay, the writer argues about the negative effects of social media use. Discuss the questions below. Then read the essay which includes an introduction, four topic sentences, and a conclusion. Develop each body paragraph with supporting information. You may write on a separate piece of paper.

  1. Are you active on social media? Which sites do you use?

  2. What are some of the advantages of being active on social media? Are there any disadvantages?

WORDS TO KNOW Essay 4.2

authentic: (adj) genuine; valid
everyday: (adj) ordinary and commonplace
inadequate: (adj) not good enough or not enough
intensify: (v) to increase, get stronger

isolation: (n) separation from others
unprecedented: (adj) never before experienced
worldwide: (adv) universally; internationally

ESSAY 4.2

Anti-Social Media?

1   How big of a role does social media play in **everyday** life? There are 2.8 billion active social media users **worldwide**, and that number keeps growing year after year. Those users may be updating their Facebook statuses, posting videos to YouTube, communicating via WhatsApp, tweeting on Twitter, or liking photos on Instagram. People today are sharing an **unprecedented** amount of information about their personal lives, but what are they really sharing? Just like the filters on Snapchat, social media allows people to present a 'reality' that is not in fact very real or **authentic.** Rather than bringing people together with all this supposed familiarity, social media can actually **intensify** feelings of **isolation**; as a result, its use should be monitored more closely.

Young women walk and talk together after school in Bangladesh. Cultivating relationships is critical in this age of social media.

2   Spending time on social media takes away time and energy that could be put toward cultivating real relationships.

_____

_____

_____

_____

3   Seeing only the best of other people's lives can make social media users feel **inadequate** and depressed.

_____

_____

_____

_____

4   Personal health can be negatively impacted by spending too much time on social media.

_____

_____

_____

_____

5   Some people might argue that messaging on social media can eventually lead to face-to-face interactions. This can be dangerous however. In reality, no one really knows if the person is conveying his or her real character.

_____

_____

_____

_____

6   Heavy users of social media are often negatively affected by it, losing their sense of value as human beings and feeling separated from the community they hoped to be a part of. Self-monitoring of social media use is the first and most important step in curbing this trend of over-using social media. That, coupled with comprehensive education programs, can lessen the dangers of too much time on social media.

ACTIVITY 4 | Writing pro and con thesis statements

Read the following list of topics for argument essays. For each topic, write a pro thesis statement and a con thesis statement. Then compare your statements with your classmates' statements.

1. **Topic: Women in the military**

    Pro thesis statement: _In a society where women are chief executive officers of companies, leaders of nations, and family breadwinners, there is no reason for them not to play an active role in the military._

    Con thesis statement: _Women should not be allowed to fight in the military because they do not have the physical strength or endurance required in combat._

2. **Topic: Driver's license age restrictions**

    Pro thesis statement: _____

    _____

    Con thesis statement: _____

    _____

3. Topic: Using animals in research

Pro thesis statement: _____

_____

Con thesis statement: _____

_____

4. Topic: Space exploration

Pro thesis statement: _____

_____

Con thesis statement: _____

_____

5. Topic: Buying paper or plastic tableware (cups, plates, forks)

Pro thesis statement: _____

_____

Con thesis statement: _____

_____

WRITER'S NOTE Focus on the Facts

Remember that an argument essay is NOT the same as an opinion essay. Argument essays focus on facts and evidence while opinion essays tend to be more personal. Because the tone of an argument essay is more formal, do NOT use "I" or "we" in this type of writing.

Using animals, such as these domestic rats, for research could lead to scientific breakthroughs.

Grammar: Controlling Tone with Modals

When you write an argument essay, you want to be aware of how your arguments sound. Are they too strong? Not strong enough? Certain words can help control the tone of an argument.

Modals can change the tone of a sentence. Modals such as *must*, *will*, and *had better* make a verb stronger. Other modals, such as *may*, *might*, *should*, *can*, *could*, and *would*, make a verb softer. Remember to use modals to strengthen or soften your verbs.

Asserting a Point

Strong modals, such as *must*, *will*, and *had better*, help writers to assert their main points. When you use these words, readers know where you stand on an issue.

> The facts clearly show that researchers **must** stop unethical animal testing.

> People who value their health **had better** stop smoking immediately.

Acknowledging an Opposing Point

Weaker modals, such as *may*, *might*, *should*, *can*, *could*, and *would*, help make an opposing opinion sound weak. You acknowledge an opposing point when you use *may*, for example, but this shows that the statement is not strong and can be easily refuted. In short, the use of *may* and *might* is crucial to constructing a proper counterargument and then refutation.

Here is an example from Activity 2. The modal within the counterargument is circled and the refutation is underlined:

> Some parents (might) disagree and claim that only academic subjects should be taught in school. Then again, most parents do not have the time or the resources to make sure that their children are getting enough exercise.

Here are more examples:

> While it (may) be true that people have eaten meat for a long time, the number one killer of Americans now is heart disease, caused in part by the consumption of animal fat.

> Certainly, some citizens (could) be against mandatory military service, but those who do serve in the military often have a strong sense of pride and personal satisfaction.

ACTIVITY 5 | Choosing modals

Read the essay about entrepreneurship, and circle the correct modal in each set of parentheses. Then answer the questions that follow.

WORDS TO KNOW Essay 4.3

accessible: (adj) easily available
capacity: (n) natural ability
commitment: (n) a promise; loyalty to a person or cause
creation: (n) the beginning of something; invention

guaranteed: (adj) certain; covered by a promise
income: (n) money earned
innovation: (n) a new idea or method
prosperity: (n) wealth; success
remark: (n) a comment; statement

Becoming a Successful Entrepreneur

1   Ludwick Marishane is not famous. However, in May 2012 he stood on the TED stage and told his success story. Ludwick had heard a casual **remark** about some people living without access to clean water. At the time, he was just a high school student in a rural community in South Africa. The information he learned drove him to find a solution to the problems caused by a lack of clean water. His research led to the **creation** of a lotion called DryBath: a way of washing without water. Ludwick Marishane became a successful entrepreneur[1] even with his limited resources (Spector, Dina. "A High School Student Invented A Bath-Substituting Lotion That Could Save Millions Of People." *Business Insider,* January 15, 2013, www.businessinsider.com/ludwick-marishane-drybath-2013-1). Is he an exception? Of course not. Regardless of what skeptics[2] **1**(can / might) say, the fact is that everyone has the **capacity** to build or create something new.

2   Most people have the creativity to come up with a new idea. It could be anything: a smartphone app, a concept to improve education, or an invention to help people in need. This creativity is the driving force needed to produce something and become a successful entrepreneur. Education levels do not matter in this case. From people with little education to those with advanced degrees, their hearts and minds **2**(might / must) be filled with imagination in order to succeed. In fact, this essential element of imagination often thrives among people who have few resources. These people tend to look at things in a different way from those who have everything given to them. It **3**(may / should) be easier to "think outside the box" when resources are not easily available. When there is a real need, the motivation to create and devise solutions is even stronger.

3   **Commitment**, not cash, is what leads to success. It is dedication that turns ideas into realities. Thomas Edison, the inventor of the light bulb, is the perfect example of someone who was committed to success. According to *Forbes* magazine, Edison tried over 1,000 times to invent a working light bulb. When he was asked how he felt about failing so many times, Edison responded, "I didn't fail 1,000 times. The light bulb was an invention with 1,000 steps." Even if resources are not easily **accessible**, a committed entrepreneur will find a way to pursue his or her ideas.

4   Some people say that opportunity only exists where there is wealth. **Prosperity**, they believe, is the key to successful entrepreneurship. They say that without proper funding, small businesses **4**(cannot / had better not) succeed. However, as stated above, the success of entrepreneurs is definitely achievable without large sums of money. Opportunity can be found anywhere. In fact, some of the most successful **innovations** have come from individuals who do not have easy access to funds. Ludwick Marishane, who had a limited **income**, became a successful entrepreneur. If the need for a product or business is there, success is practically **guaranteed**.

5   There are people who believe that entrepreneurial success is possible only for a select few. The data, however, shows a completely different reality. Like Ludwick Marishane, individuals from all over the world [5] (can / might) tap into their natural creativity and commitment, and find opportunity around them. Potential entrepreneurs [6] (could / should) show their capabilities and present their concepts to the world. Their success [7] (must / will) make the world a better place.

[1] entrepreneur: a person who creates his or her own business
[2] skeptic: someone who doubts that something is true

Entrepreneur Ludwick Marishane in Cape Town, South Africa

1. What is the thesis statement? _____

2. What are the three topic sentences in the body paragraphs that support this thesis?

_____

_____

_____

3. Would you like to be an entrepreneur? Discuss with a partner.

Counterargument and Refutation

The key to persuading the reader that your viewpoint is valid is to support it in every paragraph. However, an argument essay is not complete without one **counterargument.** Think of the counterargument as the strongest idea that someone would give you to show you that your ideas are wrong. A solid argument essay shows that you have looked at all sides of an issue carefully.

Typically, the counterargument paragraph is placed after your main arguments. After you provide the counterargument, you must show why it is not valid. This is called a **refutation**. You are presenting your opponent's idea but are also including reasons why it is not valid.

Look at the following excerpts from two argument essays in this unit. The counterarguments are in *italics* and the refutations are <u>underlined</u>.

From Essay 4.1:

Opponents of mandatory uniforms say that students who wear school uniforms cannot express their individuality. On the surface, this point has some merit. <u>However, as stated previously, school is a place to learn, not to show off wealth or style.</u>

From Essay 4.2:

Some people might argue that messaging on social media can eventually lead to face-to-face interactions. This can be dangerous however. <u>In reality, no one really knows if the person is conveying his or her real character.</u>

Note that what begins as a counterargument ends up as another reason in support of the claim.

ACTIVITY 6 | Writing counterarguments

Read the arguments. Then write a counterargument for each.

The Guam kingfisher is extinct in the wild.

1. Animals should not be kept in zoos. Counterargument:

   Some animals would die out completely if they were not cared for in captivity.

2. Schools need to replace paper books with e-books. Counterargument:

3. Everyone should learn how to drive. Counterargument:

_____

_____

4. The best way to learn a second language is to visit a foreign country. Counterargument:

_____

_____

5. People should become vegetarians because they are healthier than meat eaters. Counterargument:

_____

_____

6. Reality TV shows should be banned because they are not educational. Counterargument:

_____

_____

ACTIVITY 7 | Writing refutations

Read the counterarguments. Then write a refutation for each. The contrasting connection word or phrase has been written for you.

1. Parents of extremely young beauty pageant contestants believe that these competitive contests help build their children's confidence.

However, _____

_____

2. Many companies do not give their employees financial assistance to sign up for gym memberships or nutritional programs, stating that they are too expensive to manage.

Even though they may seem expensive, _____

_____

3. Opponents of the fast-food ban in high schools insist that students should have the freedom to eat whatever they wish.

While this may be true, _____

_____

4. Many science and math teachers continue to believe that boys are better in these subjects than girls.

In reality, _____

_____

Avoiding Faulty Logic

As a writer, you want to convince readers to agree with your arguments. If they are not logical, you will not persuade your readers. Logic can prove your point and disprove your opponent's point, and perhaps change your readers' mind about an issue. If you use faulty logic (logic not based on fact), readers will not believe you or take your position seriously.

Here are logical errors that you should avoid when writing.

Events Related Only by Sequence

When one event happens, it does not necessarily cause a second event to happen, even if one follows the other in time.

Example: Henry went to the football game, and then he had a car accident. Therefore, football games cause car accidents.

Problem: The two events may have happened in that order, but do not mislead the reader into thinking that the first action was responsible for the second.

Appeal to Authority

Using famous names may often help you prove or disprove your point. However, be sure to use the name logically and in the proper context.

Example: If she wants to pass her engineering class, she needs to buy an Apple computer because NASA uses Macs.

Problem: While NASA is one of the most famous science and technology organizations, its use of Macs does not guarantee success in a college engineering class.

Sweeping Generalizations

Words such as *all, always,* and *never* are too broad and cannot be supported.

Example: Everyone is interested in improving the quality of education.

Problem: Really? Everyone? What about a 90-year-old woman who does not have enough money to pay for her medicine? Her immediate concerns are probably not on improving education.

Hasty Generalizations (Insufficient Statistics)

Hasty generalizations are just what they sound like—making quick judgments based on inadequate or not enough information.

Example: A woman is driving through a small town. She passes three cars, all of which are white pickup trucks. She then writes in her report describing the town that everyone in this town drives a white pickup truck.

Problem: The woman only saw three vehicles. The town actually has over 300 cars. The number of cars that she saw was too small for her to come to that conclusion.

Loaded Words

Some words contain positive or negative connotations. Try to avoid them. Your readers may think you are trying to appeal to them by using these emotionally packed words. You want to persuade the reader by using logical arguments, not emotional words.

Example: The blue-flag freedom fighters won the war against the green-flag guerrillas.

Problem: The terms *freedom fighters* (positive) and *guerrillas* (negative) may influence the readers' opinion about the two groups without any support for the bias.

Either/Or Arguments

When you argue a point, be careful not to limit the outcome choices to only two. In fact, there are often a multitude of choices.

Example: Higher education has become so expensive that universities must either offer more scholarships or significantly reduce tuition rates.

Problem: This statement implies that only two choices are available to the university.

ACTIVITY 8 | Avoiding faulty logic

Read the following paragraph. The underlined words represent faulty logic. Write the kind of faulty logic above each one.

PARAGRAPH 4.1

Penny Wise

Next week, our ¹fine upstanding citizens will go to the polls to vote for or against a penny sales tax for construction of a new stadium. This law, if passed, will cause hardship for local residents, according to Senator Johnson. Our taxes are high enough as it is, so why do our city's ²apathetic leaders think that we will run happily to the polls and vote "yes"? In addition, these construction projects ³are never completed on time and always come in over budget. ⁴If we take a look at what happened to our sister city as a result of a similar bill, we will see that this new tax will have negative effects. ⁵Last year, that city raised its sales tax by one percent. Only three weeks later, there were demonstrations in the street. If we want to keep our fair city as it is, ⁶we must either vote "no" on the ballot question or live in fear of violence.

Grammar: Using the *If* Clause

The *if* clause explains a condition that is necessary for a specific outcome. It is a type of adverb clause. (You will learn more about adverb clauses in Unit 5.) Study the following examples:

TIME	*IF* CLAUSE / SITUATION	OUTCOME
General	If it **is** too hot,	we **turn on** the air conditioning.
Future real	If it **is** too hot,	**will** we **can turn on** the air conditioning. **may**
Present/ Future unreal	If the restaurant **opened** at noon, (The restaurant does not open at noon.)	**could** we **would eat** lunch there. **might**
Past unreal	If the students **had asked** questions during the lecture, (They did not ask questions during the lecture.)	**would have** they **might have understood** the concepts better. **could have**

ACTIVITY 9 | Identifying and labeling *if* clauses

Each of the following sentences contains an *if* clause. Underline the verbs in both parts of the sentence. In the space provided, identify the *if* clause as either general (G), future real (FR), present/future unreal (PFU), or past unreal (PU).

___PFU___ **1.** If the government <u>passed</u> the new law, the citizens <u>would have</u> more access to health care.

_____ **2.** If fast-food is the only option, then we eat fast-food.

_____ **3.** If we show commitment and creativity, we will become successful in whatever we do.

_____ **4.** If the storm had struck in the middle of the night, more people would have been injured.

_____ **5.** If schools adopt a 12-year fitness plan, the positive results will create an awareness of both physical fitness and communication skills.

_____ **6.** According to researchers, exercise has maximum benefit if it is done regularly.

_____ **7.** World War I could have been avoided if certain steps had been taken.

_____ **8.** We could take a break if the class started on time.

Citing Sources to Avoid Plagiarism

When writing argument essays, it is helpful to find facts, figures, or quotes to help support your ideas. With the ease of the Internet, however, writers sometimes forget to give credit to the person (or article or website) that the information came from. **Plagiarism**—whether done intentionally or unintentionally—is the act of taking others' words without properly giving credit to the source. Plagiarism is considered a very serious offense in academia and should be avoided at all costs.

After you have decided that the information you have found in a source is appropriate to support your ideas, you need to insert it in your essay correctly. There are two choices:

1. **Quoting**. If the information is not too long, you can put it in quotation marks. It is a good idea to introduce the quote with a phrase, such as *According to (name of source), "(exact words from that source)."* This way you not only acknowledge the source but also show that the information is taken word for word. Be careful, however, not to use too many quotations in any one paragraph. Remember, the reader is looking for *your* voice, not someone else's.

   Example:
   According to The American Heart Association, "Each meal should contain at least 1 fruit or vegetable."

2. **Paraphrasing**. Another method of avoiding plagiarism is to paraphrase your source's information. That is, you put the information in your own words. You still need to explain where the information came from, but you do not need to use quotation marks.

   Example:
   According to the United States' Office of Disease Prevention and Health Promotion (health. gov/dietaryguidelines), in order for a diet to be considered healthy, kids should eat at least two fruits and three vegetables every day.

Your instructor can help you if you are unsure of when, where, or exactly how to cite information. In addition, librarians and other school support services have information on methods of avoiding plagiarism. The key to using outside sources correctly is to be diligent in citing the source you use and to ask questions if you are unsure of how to complete this task. For more information, see *Citing Sources and Avoiding Plagiarism* in the *Writer's Handbook*.

WRITER'S NOTE Documenting the Source of Information

Remember to always document where you found your outside information. A good way to start is to copy and paste all Web addresses of sites you visit while you are doing research. This will get you started on the path to correctly citing your sources.

BUILDING BETTER VOCABULARY

WORDS TO KNOW

accessible (adj) AW	guaranteed (adj) AW	intensify (v) AW	punishment (n) AW
associated with (adj)	implement (v) AW	isolation (n) AW	remark (n)
authentic (adj)	inadequate (adj) AW	merit (n)	unity (n) AW
capacity (n) AW	incident (n) AW	on the surface (phr)	unprecedented (adj) AW
commitment (n) AW	income (n) AW	opponent (n)	wealth (n)
creation (n) AW	innovation (n) AW	prosperity (n)	worldwide (adv)
everyday (adj)			

ACTIVITY 10 | Word associations

Circle the word or phrase that is more closely related to the bold word or phrase on the left.

1. associated with	connected to	worse than
2. capacity	to learn a language	to rain
3. commitment	dedication	disinterest
4. implement	begin using	stop using
5. inadequate	enough	lacking
6. incident	event	surprise
7. income	entrance	money
8. merit	problem	value
9. on the surface	difficult to see	easy to see
10. punishment	negative effect	positive effect

ACTIVITY 11 | Collocations

Fill in the blank with the word that most naturally completes the phrase.

accessible	authentic	everyday	unity	unprecedented

1. a/an _____ occurrence

2. a period of _____ growth

3. a show of _____

4. a/an _____ document

5. easily _____

| guaranteed | opponent | prosperity | remark | worldwide |

6. gain _____ attention

7. a casual _____

8. satisfaction _____

9. a worthy _____

10. a period of peace and _____

ACTIVITY 12 | Word forms

Complete each sentence with the correct word form. Use the correct form of the verbs.

NOUN	VERB	ADJECTIVE	ADVERB	SENTENCES
authenticity	authenticate	authentic	authentically	**1.** Before buying the expensive purse, she wanted to make sure of its _____ . **2.** After intense examination, the Roman coins were found to be _____ .
innovation	innovate	innovative		**3.** _____ in technology has changed the way we live our lives. **4.** Young people have _____ ideas on how to improve their memory skills.
intensity	intensify	intensive	intensively	**5.** The wind _____ during the night. **6.** International students often take _____ language courses before entering university.

NOUN	VERB	ADJECTIVE	ADVERB	SENTENCES
isolation	isolate	isolated		**7.** While stranded on the island, he lived in _____ . **8.** Children with low self-esteem often _____ themselves from their classmates.
wealth		wealthy		**9.** Only _____ people go to that restaurant because it is so expensive. **10.** The accumulated _____ of the royal family is enormous.

ACTIVITY 13 | Vocabulary in writing

Choose five words from Words to Know. Write a complete sentence with each word.

1. _____

2. _____

3. _____

4. _____

5. _____

BUILDING BETTER SENTENCES

ACTIVITY 14 | Combining sentences

Combine the ideas into one sentence. You may change the word forms, but do not change or omit any ideas. There may be more than one answer.

1. One of the advantages is its price.
It is the price of the software.
The software is for computers.

_____

_____

2. Professors should remember something about students.
Students are enrolled in many classes.
The classes are different.

_____

_____

3. Some children tend to be more organized.
These children have strict parents.
Other children are less organized.

_____

_____

ACTIVITY 15 | Writing sentences

Read the pairs of words. Write an original sentence using the words listed.

1. (pollution/if) _If people do not change their consumption habits, pollution will eventually_

destroy the entire planet.

2. (if/uniforms) _____

_____

3. (university/requirements) _____

_____

4. (cell phones/rules) _____

_____

5. (should/law) _____

_____

6. (ought to/independent) _____

_____

7. (must/ideas) _____

_____

8. (parents/children) _____

_____

ACTIVITY 16 | Describing a scene

On a separate piece of paper, write three to five sentences about the photo.

Subway workers help close
the doors in Tokyo, Japan.

WRITING

ACTIVITY 17 | Planning an essay

Follow the steps below to develop ideas for an argument essay.

1. First, choose a thesis statement from the statements that you wrote in Activity 4, or choose
   any other topic and thesis statement that you want to write about. Remember that the topic
   must have more than one point of view to qualify as an argument.

   Essay topic: _____

   Thesis statement: _____

   _____

2. Now brainstorm ideas about your topic. Write everything you can think of that supports
   your argument. You may want to begin by answering this question about your thesis
   statement: *Why do I believe this?*

3. Look at your brainstorming information again. Choose three or four reasons that support
   your thesis most effectively and circle them. You now know what your major supporting
   information will be.

4. Write one counterargument and a refutation for your argument essay.

Counterargument: _____

_____

_____

Refutation: _____

_____

_____

5. Remember to include a restatement of your thesis and your opinion about the issue in your conclusion.

If you need ideas for phrasing, see *Useful Words and Phrases* in the *Writer's Handbook*.

ACTIVITY 18 | Planning with an outline

Complete the outline as a guide to help you brainstorm a more detailed plan for your argument essay. Use your ideas from Activity 17. You may need to use either more or fewer points under each heading. Write complete sentences where possible.

Topic: _____

1. Introduction (Paragraph 1)

   A. Hook: _____   _____

   B. Connecting information: _____   _____

       _____

   C. Thesis statement: _____

       _____

2. Body

   A. Paragraph 2 (first reason) topic sentence: _____

       _____

       1. _____

   SUPPORT   **2.** _____

       3. _____

B. Paragraph 3 (second reason) topic sentence: _____

_____

SUPPORT

1. _____

2. _____

3. _____

C. Paragraph 4 (third reason) topic sentence: _____

_____

SUPPORT

1. _____

2. _____

3. _____

D. Paragraph 5 (counterargument and refutation)

1. Counterargument: _____

_____

2. Refutation: _____

_____

E. Conclusion (Paragraph 6)

1. Restated thesis: _____

_____

2. Opinion: _____

_____

ACTIVITY 19 | Peer editing your outline

Exchange books with a partner. Read your partner's outline in Activity 18. Then use the Peer Editing Form for Outlines in the *Writer's Handbook* to help you comment on your partner's work. Be sure to offer positive suggestions to help your partner improve his or her writing. Consider your partner's comments as you revise your outline. Make sure you have enough information to develop your supporting sentences.

ACTIVITY 20 | Writing an argument essay

Write an essay based on your revised outline from Activity 19. Use at least two of the vocabulary words or phrases presented in the unit. Underline these words and phrases in your essay.

ACTIVITY 21 | Editing your essay

Exchange papers from Activity 20 with a partner. Read your partner's essay. Then use Peer Editing Form 4 in the *Writer's Handbook* to help you comment on your partner's writing. Consider your partner's comments as you revise your essay.

Additional Topics for Writing

Here are five ideas for an argument essay. Follow your teacher's instructions and choose one or more topics to write about.

TOPIC 1:   Look at the photo on the opening pages of this unit. Reread your freewrite. Is the growth of industry more important than nature conservation? Make a decision about this issue, and write an argument essay about industry versus nature.

TOPIC 2:   Should couples be required to take parenting classes before they decide to have a baby? Argue for or against this idea.

TOPIC 3:   Should a child be allowed to have full access to technology before the age of five? Develop a thesis statement about some aspect of an age limit for technology use and support it in your argument essay.

TOPIC 4:   Should high school students be required to pass one year of a foreign language course? Why or why not? Choose one side and write your essay in support of it.

TOPIC 5:   The media often place heavy emphasis on the opinions and actions of celebrities, such as actors and sports stars. Should we pay attention to these opinions and actions? Choose one side of this argument and write your essay in support of it.

TEST PREP

You should spend about 40 minutes on this task. Write about the following topic:

What should happen to students who are caught cheating on an exam? Why?

Be sure to include a short introduction (with a thesis statement), logical support, a counterargument, and a refutation. Give reasons for your answer and include any relevant examples from your knowledge or experience. Write at least 250 words.

TIP

Avoid information that is too general in your timed writing. Statements such as "Cheating is bad." do not give the reader anything new to think about. You want to show that you have thought about the subject and provide interesting and specific information.

---

5 | Problem-Solution Essays

OBJECTIVES
- Write a problem-solution essay
- Write complex sentences with adverb clauses
- Evaluate websites for validity

Approximately three billion people around the world cook with open fires. This has potentially deadly health and environmental consequences. An aid group helped Rosa de Sapeta in Jocotenango, Guatemala, get a clean cook stove. Now her grandchildren can join her when she cooks.

FREEWRITE | Look at the photo and read the caption. On a separate piece of paper, write your ideas about the problem: Why is it significant? Write about the solution: Is it the best? If not, offer an alternative.

ELEMENTS OF GREAT WRITING

What Is a Problem-Solution Essay?

A **problem-solution essay** is written to identify and explain a problem and offer one or more solutions. It is a very common essay type on standardized exams and in classroom assignments. While it is simple to organize, it sometimes requires doing some research.

Typically, the introductory paragraph presents the problem. This may include background information about the problem or the history of the problem: *Is this a new problem? Has the problem existed for many years?* The essay then explains why the problem is significant: *Why should the reader be concerned?* The writer must get the reader interested in the problem.

The body paragraphs offer possible solutions. The information here should explain why or how the solution will be effective. One solution can be presented with two or three points, or two or three solutions can be presented.

Finally, the concluding paragraph summarizes the points and may offer a call to action—recommendations or steps for the reader to take to help solve the problem. In summary, the problem-solution essay:

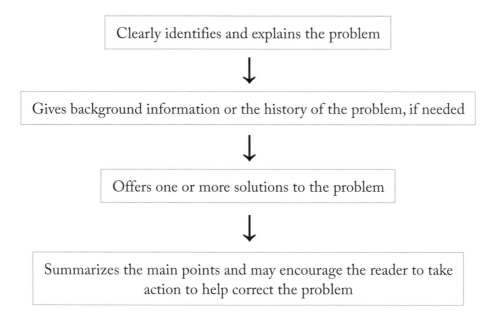

Clearly identifies and explains the problem

↓

Gives background information or the history of the problem, if needed

↓

Offers one or more solutions to the problem

↓

Summarizes the main points and may encourage the reader to take action to help correct the problem

Choosing a Topic

In a problem-solution essay, the writer may choose a topic for which there are many solutions. In this case, the writer might choose to write about the *best* solution. For instance, if the topic is the problem of too much trash going into landfills, the essay can focus on one solution: boycotting plastic products. The body paragraphs then explain how this solution will work.

On the other hand, the writer might choose to provide two or more solutions to this problem: boycotting plastic products and encouraging recycling. In this model, each solution will be a separate paragraph.

WRITER'S NOTE Focusing Your Essay

One of the most common mistakes that writers make in writing a problem-solution essay is just listing a number of problems and some solutions. Remember, focusing on one problem and one or two solutions will result in a well-developed essay with strong examples and details. After reading the essay, the reader should have a clear understanding of the issue and how the solution or solutions address it.

Organizing a Problem-Solution Essay

There are two basic ways to organize a problem-solution essay—presenting one solution or two or more solutions.

ONE SOLUTION	TWO OR MORE SOLUTIONS

Paragraph 1: Introduction
      Hook (background information or history of the problem)
      Connecting information
      Thesis statement
Paragraph 2: Why the problem is important
Paragraph 3: Solution
Paragraph 4: Conclusion
	Paragraph 1: Introduction
	      Hook (background information or history of the problem)
	      Connecting information
	      Thesis statement
	Paragraph 2: Why the problem is important
	Paragraph 3: Solution 1 (with a transition from Solution 1 to Solution 2)
	Paragraph 4: Solution 2
	Paragraph 5: Conclusion

ACTIVITY 1 | Brainstorming problem-solution topics

The following topics are all appropriate for a problem-solution essay. In pairs, choose two of the topics and complete the information on the next page. The final item should be your own original topic. One topic has been done for you.

Internet Privacy

Traffic in Our City

✓ Homeschooling: Quality Control

The Real Issue of 'Brain Drain'

Cell Phone Addiction

Trash Troubles on Mount Everest

Homesickness

Insomnia

Noise Pollution

Bad Neighbors

Trash on the Beach

Rising Sea Levels

Topic from list: _____Homeschooling: Quality Control_____

1. Why is this problem important?

    Educators want to be sure that a homeschooling curriculum covers the same information

    as traditional curricula.

2. What are two possible solutions to this problem?

    Solution 1: _Create a list of required content that homeschooled children must learn._

    Solution 2: _Require training for homeschool parents to ensure that the content is_

    delivered according to standards.

Topic from list: _____

1. Why is this problem important? _____

    _____

2. What is the best possible solution to this problem?

    Solution: _____

    _____

Topic from list: _____

1. Why is this problem important? _____

    _____

2. What are two possible solutions to this problem?

    Solution 1: _____

    _____

    Solution 2: _____

    _____

Original topic: _____

1. Why is this problem important? _____

    _____

2. What are two possible solutions to this problem?

Solution 1: _____

_____

Solution 2: _____

_____

ACTIVITY 2 | Analyzing a problem-solution essay

Read the problem-solution essay. Then answer the questions that follow.

> **WORDS TO KNOW** Essay 5.1
>
> **automatically:** (adv) functioning by itself
> **budget:** (n) a financial plan; money for a particular purpose
> **generate:** (v) to produce, create
> **integrity:** (n) strong morals; honesty
> **keep track of:** (phr v) to follow the progress of something, monitor
>
> **measure:** (n) a procedure, method
> **prominent:** (adj) well-known, famous
> **trustworthy:** (adj) dependable; honest
> **usage:** (n) use
> **widespread:** (adj) covering a large area

ESSAY 5.1

Safeguarding Internet Privacy

1   *Time* magazine recently reported that—worldwide—more than three billion people use the Internet. Internet **usage** has increased exponentially[1], from metropolitan hubs to rural areas in developing countries. As with most other advances, along with the benefits come the dangers. One of the most **widespread** dangers has to do with maintaining individual Internet privacy. The risk here is that personal data can be misused on the Internet. Although the danger is real, there are certain ways for individuals to protect their private information.

[1]exponentially: more and more rapidly

An Internet cafe in Prague, Czech Republic

129

2 The issue of Internet privacy has gained attention over the last few years. Recently, one of the most **prominent** technology companies in the world, Facebook, came under fire[2] when it was discovered that its users' data was made available to outside companies (third-party companies) without users' knowledge. It worked as follows: Facebook users would log in to a different app—such as an online game or shopping site—using their Facebook login information. When these users clicked on "agree" to use the app, that company immediately gained access to all of the users' Facebook information. Then, depending on the **integrity** of the company, that same information could be illegally sold to third parties, sometimes for as little as $5.00 per login. By this time, users' private information had traveled to various companies, with most users unaware of this cycle. At best, this stolen personal information can mean a lot of unwanted advertising; at worst, it can lead to identity theft and stolen assets.

3 One way that Internet users can protect their privacy is to hide their surfing habits. This is an option that is available on all major Web browsers, free of charge. Private browsing deletes temporary Internet files, browsing history, and cookies (small files that hold data connected to a website) when users end their Internet session. This, in turn, limits companies' access to personal information and website preferences. The less these companies know, the less direct marketing clutter will appear on users' social media, email, and so on. Another way to achieve the same effect is to use a Web proxy, or VPN (Virtual[3] Private Network). A VPN hides the user's IP address, so when an Internet surfer visits a website, that particular website cannot see where the search is coming from. It is similar to using a longer, more complicated route to get to a final destination. Instead of the direct highway (the actual IP address) of a computer surfer, the company sees a different road.

4 Using password managers is another possible solution; password managers protect sensitive information and make it more difficult to hack. Computer users are told again and again to use different passwords for different accounts, but this rule is often not followed. A password manager **generates** unique passwords for websites that require a login. Not only that, but the password manager **keeps track of** logins and offers assistance if a user gets confused or forgets certain passwords. Instead of trying to remember email logins, usernames, and passwords, the user needs to type only one master password into the password manager, and the manager does the rest, **automatically** filling in all of the required information. Password managers are priced from completely free to approximately $50.00. Whatever one's **budget**, there is a password manager to protect sensitive information.

5 These simple tools can be the difference between a safe Web-surfing experience and a serious threat to Internet privacy. There is no excuse for not taking advantage of these simple tools. They are easy to use, free or inexpensive, and completely **trustworthy**. The next time Internet users complain about a computer security issue, they should be reminded that the safety **measures** were always there, ready to use.

[2]come under fire: be criticized
[3]virtual: computer generated

1. What is the main purpose of this essay? Begin with *The purpose is...*

   _____

   _____

2. What is the thesis statement? Write it here. _____

   _____

3. In Paragraph 2, the author gives details about the importance of Internet privacy. Why is Internet privacy important? _____

   _____

4. What are the two specific solutions presented in the body of the essay? _____

   _____

5. Reread the concluding paragraph of Essay 5.1. What is the call to action? _____

   _____

Developing a Problem-Solution Essay

Outlines are useful methods of organizing the information in an essay. Outlines usually contain the main ideas followed by details that will be included within each paragraph. Read this dictionary entry for 'brain drain' before completing an outline on the topic.

---

brain drain (noun) [singular]

a situation in which many educated or professional people leave one place or profession and move to another one that gives them better pay or living conditions

- Nothing has been done to stop the *brain drain* of health care providers as more and more doctors and nurses are taking jobs in other countries.

Nurses in Manila wait to take their medical oath after passing their exams. Filipino nurses are in high demand in the United States.

ACTIVITY 3 | Outlining a problem-solution essay

Read the outline for a problem-solution essay about brain drain. The outline is missing some important information. Use the words and phrases from the box to fill in the missing pieces.

research opportunities	call to action	thesis statement
engineering	restate the thesis statement	low salaries
definition	✔ the real issue of brain drain	

Title: _The Real Issue of Brain Drain_____

I. Paragraph 1: Introduction

   A. Hook

   B. _____

   C. Background information

   D. _____

II. Paragraph 2: Why and how it's a problem

   A. Western companies in search of highly skilled workers

      1. Health care

      2. _____

      3. Technology sector

   B. Limited job opportunities in native country

      1. Overqualified professionals in native countries

      2. _____

III. Paragraph 3: Solution

   A. Governmental buy-in

      1. Increased salaries

      2. More _____

   B. Private sector buy-in

      1. Foreign investment within the country

      2. More competition (no more state monopolies)

IV. Paragraph 4: Conclusion

A. _____

B. _____

Grammar: Adverb Clauses

Sentence variety is an important element in academic writing. Experienced writers do not rely on one sentence type, such as compound sentences, but instead try to use a variety of sentence types within a paragraph and essay. One way to add variety is by using complex sentences with **adverb clauses.**

An adverb clause is a dependent clause that indicates time, reason, concession, contrast, condition, purpose, or refutation. An adverb clause begins with a connector called a **subordinating conjunction**, such as *after*, *although*, *if*, *since*, and *when*. In the following sentences, the subordinating conjunctions are circled and the adverb clauses are underlined. Note that when the adverb clause begins the sentence, it is followed by a comma.

(Although) Brazil and the United States are unique countries, there are remarkable similarities in their size, ethnic diversity, and core values.

Lenient parents will not become angry or scream (if) a child screams.

(When) the Northeast is experiencing snowstorms, cities like Houston, Texas can have temperatures over 85 degrees Fahrenheit.

The workers will go on strike (unless) their demands are met.

FUNCTION	SUBORDINATING CONJUNCTIONS		EXAMPLE
time	after as as soon as before	until when whenever while	**As soon as** the lecture ended, the students left the auditorium.
reason / cause	because since		**Because** the class ran long, they did not have time to get lunch.
concession / counterargument	although even though though		**Though** some might argue that messaging on social media can lead to face-to-face interactions, there is no data to support this claim.
contrast	although even though	while	**Although** punctuation is ignored in texting, it is important in academic writing.
condition	even if if provided that	unless when	**If** more people cared about the environment, there would be far less pollution.
purpose	in order that so that		Good writers add examples **so that** their points are clear.
refutation	despite the fact that		The presentation was not rescheduled **despite the fact that** most students could not attend it.

ACTIVITY 4 | Identifying adverb clauses and subordinating conjunctions

Each sentence contains an adverb clause. Underline the adverb clause and circle the subordinating conjunction. Finally, write *S* above the subject of the adverb clause and *V* above the verb in the adverb clause.

1. (While) many marketers say there is nothing wrong with this sharing of information, very often it falls into the wrong hands.

2. Because password managers generate unique passwords for every website that is used, the user's privacy is maintained.

3. The password manager keeps track of logins and offers assistance if a user gets confused.

4. VPNs hide the user's address so that online companies cannot see the path used to reach their websites.

5. Even though password managers might seem too costly, they are available in all price ranges.

6. Despite the fact that they are easily available, many people do not take advantage of these tools.

7. Private browsing deletes temporary Internet files, browsing history, and cookies when users end their Internet session.

8. Although the danger is real, there are certain ways for individuals to protect their private information.

ACTIVITY 5 | Writing sentences using adverb clauses

Choose five words or phrases from the box and write original sentences. Be sure that each sentence includes an adverb clause.

although	whereas	until
as soon as	if	when
before	unless	while

1. _____

2. _____

3. _____

4. _____

5. _____

ACTIVITY 6 | Analyzing a problem-solution essay

Read the problem-solution essay. Then answer the questions that follow.

WORDS TO KNOW Essay 5.2

accumulate: (v) to add up, increase gradually
collaboration: (n) a partnership; working together
disposal: (n) removal; the process of getting rid of something
enforce: (v) to make people obey; apply
official: (n) an authority in an organization; officer

propose: (v) to make a suggestion
recognition: (n) praise for doing something well
regulation: (n) a rule (usually from government or other organization)
resource: (n) a supply; available amount
use up: (phr v) to consume, deplete

Yaks, or long-haired wild oxen, contribute to the trash problem on Mount Everest.

ESSAY 5.2

The Great Mount Everest Clean-Up Effort

1   Sir Edmund Hillary made history on May 29, 1953. The New Zealand native gained **recognition** as the first climber to reach the summit of Mount Everest in the Himalaya Mountains of Nepal. At that time the feat seemed almost impossible, yet, as the years went by, more and more climbers achieved the same goal. In 2017 alone, 648 adventurers successfully climbed Mount Everest. Along with an increase in the number of Everest mountain climbers is the increased problem of litter left behind on this natural wonder. Fortunately, Nepalese **officials** are working to fix this potential environmental disaster.

2   It is true that Mount Everest has brought much-needed income to Nepal, but it is also true that a lot of waste has **accumulated** as a result. Hikers require a lot of equipment to successfully climb the mountain. A typical team of hikers can easily **use up** hundreds of oxygen cylinders and as many as 15 plastic tents and other equipment during the climb. In addition, there is the issue of human waste. This has been a growing problem and has reached life-threatening levels. The waste problem now extends from the base camp to the watershed below, polluting the local water supply. Not only does all this waste ruin the beauty of what was once an unspoiled peak, but the risk of disease to Mount Everest communities grows with each passing year. In 2014, the Nepalese government tried to solve this pollution issue by implementing a law stating that climbers must bring back 18 pounds of garbage on their way down the mountain. This solution did not work for a number of reasons, especially logistics[1]. Officials hope that new strategies prove more successful.

3   A combined effort between Mount Everest officials and the city of Kathmandu has been **proposed**. Garbage **disposal** sites have been installed along the mountain paths. These sites are sturdy enough to survive yaks rummaging—or digging through—the garbage. Because the animals would destroy plastic bins, the new containers are made out of stone. In addition, heavy fines will be given to hikers who pollute the mountain. These hikers risk losing their $4,000 waste deposit if they are caught throwing things on the mountain. In this way, the careless throwing away of items will definitely be reduced. The final step is removing the garbage from the mountain. This is where a local airline comes in. It has agreed to transport the waste from the mountain to the capital city, where it will be recycled. This increased **collaboration** is bound to have a positive effect on the environmental problem.

4   The problem of environmental waste on Mount Everest is serious, with more and more climbers leaving a nasty stain on the natural beauty of the mountain. Now, with these new **regulations** in place, the mountain should see a return to its former self. There are no more excuses as the government has provided adequate **resources** to reduce pollution on the mountain. The world's highest peak deserves to be visited, but as with all wonders of the world, it should be respected. As a local Nepalese school official stated, "Tourists are not fully abiding by our rules. It is time to **enforce** the law."

[1]logistics: the organization of complicated tasks

The Himalaya Mountains have nine of the ten highest peaks in the world, including the highest: Mount Everest.

1. What is the main purpose of this essay? Begin with *The purpose is...*

_____

_____

2. What type of hook is used in this essay? _____

3. What is the thesis statement? _____

_____

4. According to the author, why is pollution on Mount Everest a serious problem?

_____

_____

Where did you find the answer? _____

5. Review Paragraph 3. The topic sentence states that the best solution is to have a combined effort between the officials of Mount Everest and the city of Kathmandu. What are the three specific actions presented in the paragraph?

_____

_____

_____

6. Review the final quote in the concluding paragraph. Rewrite it in your own words.

_____

_____

_____

BUILDING BETTER VOCABULARY

WORDS TO KNOW

accumulate (v) AW	integrity (n) AW	regulation (n) AW
automatically (adv) AW	keep track of (phr v)	resource (n) AW
budget (n)	measure (n)	trustworthy (adj)
collaboration (n)	official (n)	usage (n) AW
disposal (n) AW	prominent (adj) AW	use up (phr v)
enforce (v) AW	propose (v)	widespread (adj) AW
generate (v) AW	recognition (n)	

ACTIVITY 7 | Word associations

Circle the word or phrase that is more closely related to the bold word or phrase on the left.

1. budget	financial	intellectual
2. collaboration	alone	together
3. enforce	laws	recipes
4. generate	travel	ideas
5. keep track of	count	dismiss
6. prominent	famous	honest
7. propose	fires	solutions
8. recognition	concept	acknowledgement
9. resource	housework	online database
10. usage	common	avoidable

ACTIVITY 8 | Collocations

Fill in the blank with the word or phrase that most naturally completes the phrase.

automatically	enforce	measures	official	regulations

1. appropriate _____

2. _____ the rules

3. _____ language

4. shut down _____

5. comply with _____

| budget | disposal | integrity | trustworthy | use up |

6. _____ resources

7. reduced _____

8. a/an _____ source

9. defend one's _____

10. have at one's _____

ACTIVITY 9 | Word forms

Complete each sentence with the correct word form. Use the correct form of the verbs.

NOUN	VERB	ADJECTIVE	ADVERB	SENTENCES
accumulation	accumulate			**1.** The _____ of plastic in our oceans is frightening. **2.** It is easy to _____ a lot of unnecessary items.
collaboration	collaborate	collaborative	collaboratively	**3.** They worked _____ on the project. **4.** Without _____, the assignment will not get done.
generation	generate	generated		**5.** Today's light bulbs _____ more light than in the past. **6.** The _____ of jobs was crucial to the campaign's success.
prominence		prominent	prominently	**7.** The Academy Award show was _____ advertised weeks before the event. **8.** The Roosevelts were a _____ family in the United States in the first half of the 20th century.
proposal	propose	proposed		**9.** The mayor's _____ to solve the crime problem is solid. **10.** The faculty_____ a change to the grading system.

ACTIVITY 10 | Vocabulary in writing

Choose five words from Words to Know. Write a complete sentence with each word.

1. _____

2. _____

3. _____

4. _____

5. _____

BUILDING BETTER SENTENCES

ACTIVITY 11 | Editing from teacher comments

Read the teacher's comments. Then make the corrections.

sing/plur

One of the biggest <u>problem</u> facing children today is the number of advertisements they are

P   *frag—where is the verb?*

exposed to. In one <u>year children</u> can see tens of thousands of ads. <u>Television responsible</u> for most

advertisements targeting children. Some studies suggest that the more advertisements a child

watches, the more he or she will want material products like toys or other things <u>("9 Negative

Good! You added a source in your paper.

Side Effects of Advertising on Children." *MomJunction*, March 16, 2017, www.momjunction.

com/articles/negative-side-effects-of-advertising-on-your-children_00385891/#gref.).</u> Of course,

excellent vocab   S-V agreement

children cannot figure out the honesty of an ad because they are too <u>naïve</u>. <u>Parents has been

redundant

worrying</u> about this for many years now and want <u>real and not imaginary solutions</u> to this problem.

contraction   *sp*

If the government <u>won't</u> regulate marketing to kids, then parents will need to get more <u>involved</u>.

ACTIVITY 12 | Combining sentences

Combine the ideas into one sentence. You may change the word forms, but do not change or omit any ideas. There may be more than one answer.

1. It was exhausting.

The hikers made it to the summit.

It was the summit of the mountain.

_____

_____

2. The tech equipment is old.

The tech equipment is bulky.

The tech equipment is difficult to use.

The tech equipment is in the computer lab.

_____

_____

3. Biomedical engineering is an industry.

Biomedical engineering is fast growing.

This is especially true in Western Europe.

_____

_____

Delanie Gallagher, 10, gets her robotic prosthesis put on by engineering students Ian Palte and Mark Sullivan in the biomaterials lab at Washington University School of Medicine in St. Louis, Missouri, USA.

ACTIVITY 13 | Writing sentences

Read the pairs of words. Write an original sentence using the words listed.

1. (storm/because)_____

_____

2. (medical doctor/integrity) _____

_____

3. (even though/solution) _____

_____

4. (success/collaboration)_____

_____

5. (as long as/problem) _____

_____

6. (resources/use up) _____

_____

Developing Ideas for Writing: Choosing the Right Topic

If you are given a problem-solution essay to write and you must choose your own topic, remember these guidelines.

1. **The essay should be about a general or relatable problem.** Topics that are too personal in nature (e.g., I am always fighting with my sister. What are some solutions?) may not be interesting to the reader.
2. **The essay should have at least one solution.** If the topic is avoiding death, there is really no solution to speak of.
3. **The topic should be one about which you can easily find some basic information.** If the topic is the lack of selection at your local grocery store, you are unlikely to find much information about it.

WRITING

ACTIVITY 14 | Working with a topic

Complete the following steps to develop ideas for a problem-solution essay.

1. Choose one topic from the list below or use your own idea for a topic. If you want to use an original idea, talk to your teacher to see if it is appropriate for a problem-solution essay.

Cheating on exams	Fear of success	High cost of living
Diabetes in children	Overpopulation in urban areas	Excessive emphasis on beauty (plastic surgery)

2. Use any brainstorming method that works for you to come up with ideas about the topic. You may ask yourself questions about the topic, create a clustering diagram, make a list, or complete an outline to generate ideas.

3. Based on the ideas from your brainstorming activity, decide if you are going to present one or two solutions to the problem. What can help you make that decision?

WRITER'S NOTE Evaluating Websites

The Internet can be an excellent resource for research. But it is important to remember you cannot trust everything you read or see there. Ask yourself these questions to determine the trustworthiness of a website and its information.

1. **Authority:** Who are the authors? What are their credentials or affiliations? Which organization does this website represent? Is there a link that explains what this person or company does?

2. **Accuracy:** Are there linked sources where the information can be verified? Are the facts properly cited?

3. **Objectivity:** Is the company or person trying to sell something? Is it difficult to distinguish the content from any advertisements on the site? Is the goal or objective of the site clear?

4. **Currency:** When was the information posted? When was it last updated? Are the links up-to-date?

ACTIVITY 15 | Analyzing website information

1. Write your topic from Activity 14 here. Do an Internet search on your topic.

_____

2. Choose one of the websites that is generated. What is the name of the website?

_____

3. What is the URL of the website? _____

4. What is the extension? .org   .com   .gov   .edu   .web   other: _____

5. Who is responsible for this website? A company? An individual? A government organization?

_____

6. Is there contact information for this website?   Yes   No

7. Is there an author? _____ If yes, is it easy to find his/her name?   Yes   No

8. If an author is listed, does the website give extra information about him/her?   Yes   No

9. Does the information link to other sources/references?   Yes   No

10. Is there a date stamp on the article?   Yes   No

11. Are the advertisements clearly separated from the content?   Yes   No

12. In your opinion, what is the purpose of this website? _____

Is this website trustworthy enough to use for information about your topic? _____

Explain your answer. _____

_____

_____

_____

ACTIVITY 16 | Creating an outline

Use the following outline and your notes from Activity 14 to help you brainstorm a more detailed plan for your problem-solution essay. For this activity, use the two-solution model.

Topic: _____

I. Introduction (Paragraph 1)

    A. Hook: _____

    _____

    B. Background information or history: _____

    _____

    _____

    C. Thesis statement: _____

    _____

II. Body

    A. Paragraph 2 (Explanation of the problem): _____

    _____

    SUPPORT

    1. _____

    2. _____

    B. Paragraph 3 (Solution 1 topic sentence): _____

    _____

    SUPPORT

    1. _____

    _____

       a. _____

       b. _____

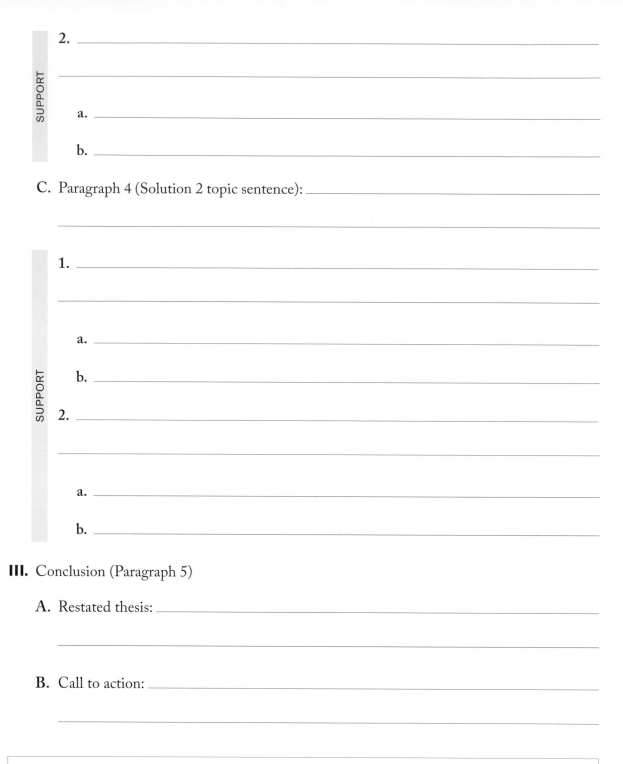

SUPPORT

2. _____

_____

    a. _____

    b. _____

C. Paragraph 4 (Solution 2 topic sentence): _____

_____

SUPPORT

1. _____

_____

    a. _____

    b. _____

2. _____

_____

    a. _____

    b. _____

III. Conclusion (Paragraph 5)

A. Restated thesis: _____

_____

B. Call to action: _____

_____

WRITER'S NOTE How Many Paragraphs Does an Essay Have?

In some writing classes, the instructor may ask for a five-paragraph essay. The five-paragraph essay consists of a clear beginning, a body of three paragraphs, and a conclusion. However, an essay can have as few as three paragraphs and as many as ten (or more) paragraphs, as long as there is a clear beginning, a body, and a conclusion. The content of the essay, not the type of writing, determines the number of paragraphs that a particular essay has.

ACTIVITY 17 | Peer editing your outline

Exchange books with a partner and look at Activity 16. Read your partner's outline. Then use the Peer Editing Form for Outlines in the *Writer's Handbook* to help you comment on your partner's work. Be sure to offer positive suggestions and comments that will help your partner write a better outline and essay. Use your partner's feedback to revise your own outline.

ACTIVITY 18 | Writing a problem-solution essay

Write a problem-solution essay based on your revised outline from Activity 17. Use at least five adverb clauses in the essay and underline them. Refer to *Steps in the Writing Process* in the *Writer's Handbook*.

ACTIVITY 19 | Editing your essay

Exchange papers from Activity 18 with a partner. Read your partner's essay. Then use Peer Editing Form 5 in the *Writer's Handbook* to help you comment on your partner's writing. Consider your partner's comments as you revise your essay.

Additional Topics for Writing

Here are five ideas for a problem-solution essay. Follow your teacher's instructions and choose one or more topics to write about.

TOPIC 1: Endangered Species

TOPIC 2: Noise Pollution

TOPIC 3: Disappearance of Languages and Cultures

TOPIC 4: Extreme Shyness

TOPIC 5: Illiteracy

TEST PREP

You should spend about 40 minutes on this task. Write a problem-solution essay about the following topic:

The lack of motivation in high school students

For this assignment, write four paragraphs: (1) introduction + thesis statement, (2) explanation of the importance of the problem, (3) the best solution to the problem, and (4) the conclusion. Write at least 250 words.

> **TIP**
> Stay away from general or vague vocabulary. Words such as *nice, good,* and *very* are too general in some contexts. Whenever possible, be more specific in your word choice.

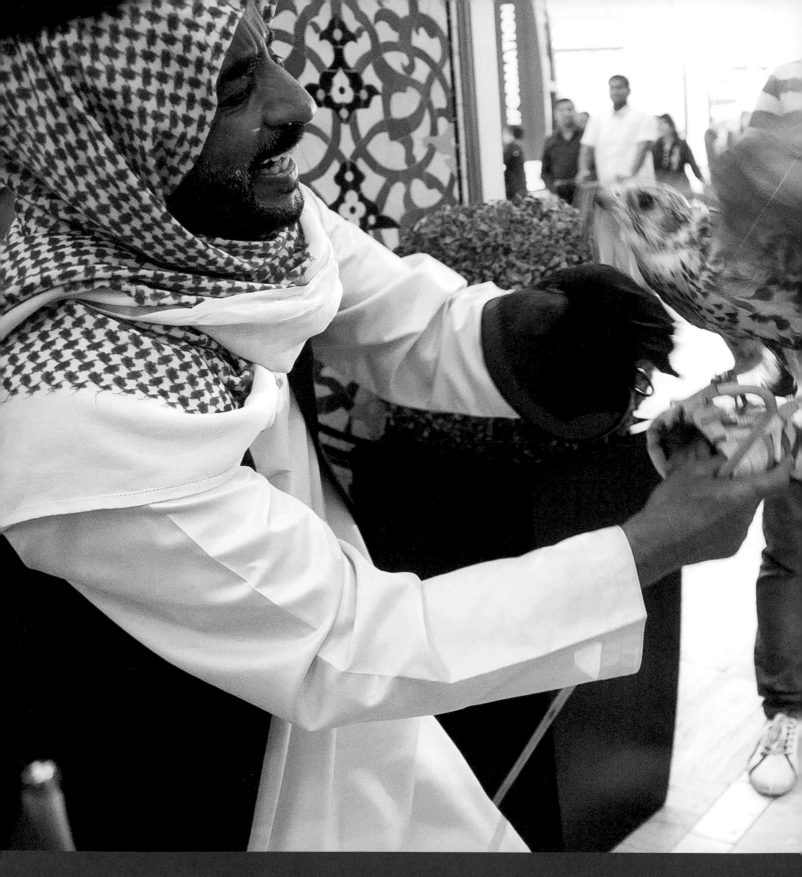

OBJECTIVES
- Write a reaction essay
- Learn how to answer short-answer exam questions
- Use adjective clause reductions correctly in an essay

6 | Reaction Essays and Exam Questions

A boy gets close with a falcon at a cultural event in the Dubai Mall in Dubai, UAE.

FREEWRITE | Look at the photo and read the caption. What does it make you think about? How does the photo make you feel? What is your reaction to this photo? Write your reaction on a separate piece of paper.

ELEMENTS OF GREAT WRITING

What Is a Reaction Essay?

A very common type of writing task—one that appears in every academic discipline—is a **reaction essay**. This can also be called a **response essay**. In a reaction essay, the writer is usually given a "prompt"—a visual or written stimulus—to think about and then respond to. Common prompts or stimuli are quotes, pieces of literature, photos, paintings, multimedia presentations, and news events. A reaction essay focuses on the writer's feelings, opinions, and personal observations about the prompt. Your task in writing a reaction essay is twofold: to briefly summarize the prompt and to give your personal reaction to it.

Pattern of Organization

When you are writing a reaction essay, the organizational pattern will look like this:

Paragraph 1	Introduction Summary of prompt and thesis statement
Paragraph 2	Your first reaction or response
Paragraph 3	Your second reaction or response
Paragraph 4	Conclusion Summary of your reaction to prompt May include a statement about prompt's impact on you

ACTIVITY 1 | Analyzing a reaction essay

Read the reaction essay, which includes an explanation of the organization. Then answer the questions that follow.

WORDS TO KNOW Essay 6.1

admiration: (n) an appreciation; high opinion
advance: (n) a development or improvement; breakthrough
alter: (v) to modify, change
courageous: (adj) brave, fearless
device: (n) a machine; mechanism

impressed: (adj) amazed
outcome: (n) a result
passionate: (adj) enthusiastic; adoring
perseverance: (n) consistent and determined effort to achieve a goal

---

The Introduction

- Clearly describes or summarizes the prompt or what you are responding to
- States the title and author of the work if responding to a particular work
- Contains the thesis statement (usually the last sentence in this paragraph)

Body

- Includes a topic sentence that states the first reaction
- Includes supporting details
- May include details from the original prompt (quotes, ideas, visuals, etc.)

Paralympic Athletes

In the article *Athletes Who Have Competed in Both the Olympics and Paralympics* (olympics.time.com/2012/09/03/before-oscar-pistorius-athletes-who-have-competed-in-both-the-olympics-and-paralympics/), Kharunya Paramaguru focuses on the many athletes with disabilities who have competed in the Olympic Games. She provides a brief history of athletes with disabilities, their achievements, and the trend of even more athletes with disabilities competing in the Olympics in the future. This article was particularly impactful to me in highlighting that athletes with disabilities are highly skilled, world-class competitors.

I was surprised to learn just how many athletes with disabilities have competed in the traditional Olympics (not the Paralympics) over the years. The Paralympic Games were created in 1948 to give athletes with disabilities the opportunity to compete. However, some gymnasts, swimmers, and track-and-field athletes with disabilities still choose to compete in the traditional Olympic Games. When the article mentioned Jeff Float, a young swimmer who was deaf but was nevertheless able to hear the shouting of the crowd at the Olympics, I was filled with awe and **admiration**. I had a similar reaction reading about Marla Runyan, a legally blind track-and-field competitor who won gold medals in the Paralympics in the 100-meter race and the long jump and went on to compete in the Olympics. Table tennis player Natalia Partyka, born without a right hand and forearm, participated in both the Olympics and the Paralympics in the same year. Her **perseverance** is to be applauded.

Body
- Includes a topic sentence stating the second reaction
- Includes supporting details

The Conclusion
- Includes your overall reaction to the prompt
- States whether the prompt had an effect or impact on you personally

I was also **impressed** to learn that athletes with disabilities have been competing in the Olympic Games for over 100 years. These athletes did not wait for a special Olympics to be created for them; they just went out and competed against their peers. Sometimes, they even won—like the gymnast George Eyser in 1904 who won several gold medals even though he had a wooden leg. This was before modern prostheses[1], such as carbon fiber blades that allow double amputees to run, and other technological **advances**.

In the end, I am inspired to learn about such **courageous** individuals who just want to compete. They are just as **passionate** about their sport as other professional athletes—maybe even more so. One **outcome** of reading this article is that my ideas about people with disabilities and their capacity to compete as athletes were **altered**. I now feel that, with the development of prostheses and other **devices**, it may not be long until all athletes, with or without disabilities, can face each other in the same space.

[1]prosthesis: (plural: prostheses) an artificial body part

Athletes participating in the 2016 Paralympic Games in Rio de Janeiro, Brazil

1. What is the thesis statement of the essay?

   _____

   _____

2. Reread the introduction. What important background information is given in this paragraph?

   _____

3. Why does the writer include the URL in the introduction paragraph?

   _____

4. How would you describe the writer's reaction to the article?

   _____

5. Read the last sentence in the conclusion. What type of conclusion does the writer offer?

   _____

WRITER'S NOTE Writing Observations

When responding to a written text, writers often highlight the most interesting parts and write down their observations. This helps them focus on the thought-provoking elements of the prompt. These notes are helpful in developing the central idea of a reaction essay.

ACTIVITY 2 | Analyzing a reaction essay

The next essay is a reaction to a photo. Discuss the questions below. Then read the reaction essay and answer the questions that follow.

1. Are you afraid of heights?
2. What is the tallest building you have ever been in? How did you feel?
3. Study the photo on the next page. Write down some notes about your emotions and reactions to it.

WORDS TO KNOW Essay 6.2

accomplish: (v) to complete, finish
comfortably: (adv) restfully; in a relaxed way
competently: (adv) done well, proficiently
construction: (n) the act of building something, typically a large structure
portray: (v) to show; describe
reminder: (n) something that helps someone to remember

represent: (v) to symbolize, signify
safety: (n) protection, security
specifically: (adv) particularly; especially
structure: (n) a building of any kind; any architectural object
visible: (adj) able to be seen

Reaction to "Old-Timer Structural Worker"

1   The photo, an image of an older structural worker, was taken around 1930 during the **construction** of a building in New York City. The **structure** that the builder is working on still stands; it is the world-famous Empire State Building, which is 102 stories tall. The black-and-white photo is a bit grainy[1], but the subject and the background are clearly **visible**. The other tall building in the photo is the well-known Chrysler Building, which is another New York landmark. For me, this photo is a symbol of hard work and hopefulness.

2   The photo **portrays** a man who is focused on his job. He is positioned high up in the air, yet he sits **comfortably** while completing his task. The man's body language shows a clear interest in doing his job **competently**. Incredibly, he is not connected to a harness or any other equipment to ensure his **safety**. The look on his face tells the story of a man with so much experience in his craft that he is not afraid of anything. What is clear is the level of comfort he shows in the photo: comfort in his surroundings despite being on an open platform over 50 stories high, and comfort in his abilities.

3   The photo also **represents** a time of hope and even optimism in the face of hard times. Looking past the man and into the horizon, one is drawn to the countless buildings in the distance. The photo speaks to me, saying, "Despite the economic depression of the time, the city is still growing." I **specifically** admire this human-made tower, which is reaching toward the sky and toward the future. The photo is a **reminder** of what people can create given their optimism and hard work.

4   It is difficult for this photo to not cause a reaction, even nearly 90 years after it was taken. The visions of society and the promise of a prosperous future are contained in "Old-Timer Structural Worker." It is a decades-old photo that reminds us of how much we have **accomplished** in a short period of time.

[1]grainy: not smooth; having a rough or gravelly quality

1. What is the main purpose of the essay? Begin with *The purpose is...*

_____

2. How was the introduction helpful for the reader?

_____

_____

3. What two main features of the photo did the writer respond to?

_____

_____

4. What is your reaction to the photo after reading the essay?

_____

_____

Developing a Reaction Essay

ACTIVITY 3 | Outlining a reaction essay

Reread Essay 6.2 and complete the outline with the missing information.

Title: _____

I. Introduction (Paragraph 1)

    A. Summary:

        1. The photo was taken around 1930.

        2. _____

        3. The Chrysler Building can be seen in the photo.

    B. Thesis: _____

II. Body

    A. Paragraph 2 (first reaction topic sentence) The photo portrays a man who is focused on his job.

        1. His body language shows that he wants to do his job well.

        2. Safety? _____

        3. He is comfortable with _____ and _____.

B. Paragraph 3 (second reaction topic sentence) _____

   1. The buildings in the background _____

   2. This human-made tower _____

   3. _____

III. Conclusion (Paragraph 4)

   A. Restated thesis: _____

   _____

   B. Opinion: _____

WRITER'S NOTE Writing Subjectively

Reaction essays express a subjective point of view. As a result, writers are free to use the first and second person. In fact, phrases such as "I think" or "I believe" are encouraged in this type of writing. Even if your reaction is negative, feel free to express your ideas.

WRITING

ACTIVITY 4 | Choosing your prompt

You will write a four-paragraph reaction essay responding to a prompt or stimulus. Choose one of the following five topics.

In this photo taken by Quang Nguyen Vinh, two women sew fishing nets in a fishing village in Vinh Hy Bay, Vietnam.

TOPIC 1: Use the photo on page 156, or find a photo that has an impact on you. Write down the name of the photo (if possible), the photographer, and where you found the photo. Describe how it makes you feel. Each paragraph should include one emotion.

TOPIC 2: Choose an article that is no longer than 400 words. In the first paragraph, summarize the most important information: the name of the article, the author, the main points of the article, and the URL (refer to the introduction of Essay 6.1 as an example). Include a thesis statement that gives your reaction to the article.

TOPIC 3: Find the advice column of a newspaper, where readers seek advice about their problems. Often the problems are personal, involving family or relationships. Choose one of the problems and write a response to it. Remember to state the nature of the problem in the introduction and to include a thesis that explains your advice.

TOPIC 4: Write a reaction to a film. Include the name of the film, the year of its release, and (preferably) the director's name. The introduction should also include a brief plot or storyline of the film so that readers who have not seen it will understand your reaction. Your body paragraphs may discuss your reaction to the acting, the storyline, the graphics, character development, or cinematography. Do not write about all of these things: choose only two (one for each paragraph).

TOPIC 5: Watch a short documentary (no longer than 30 minutes). Begin your reaction with a summary of the program in the introductory paragraph. In the following paragraphs, write a response to what you saw. How did you feel about this program? Did you agree or disagree with it? What reaction did you have after watching it?

ACTIVITY 5 | Planning with an outline

Complete the outline as a guide to help you develop a more detailed plan for your reaction essay. Write in complete sentences where possible.

Title: _____

  I. Introduction (Paragraph 1)

    A. Summary of what you are reacting to: _____

    _____

    _____

    _____

    _____

    B. Thesis statement: _____

    _____

II. Body

    A. Paragraph 2 (first reaction topic sentence): _____

    _____

SUPPORT

        1. Details and explanations _____

        _____

        2. _____

        _____

        3. _____

        _____

    B. Paragraph 3 (second reaction topic sentence) _____

SUPPORT

        1. Details and explanations _____

        _____

        2. _____

        _____

        3. _____

        _____

III. Conclusion (Paragraph 4):

    A. Restated thesis: _____

    _____

    B. Opinion: _____

    _____

ACTIVITY 6 | Peer editing your outline

Exchange books with a partner and look at Activity 5. Read your partner's outline. Then use the Peer Editing Form for Outlines in the *Writer's Handbook* to help you comment on your partner's work. Use your partner's feedback to revise your outline.

ACTIVITY 7 | Writing a reaction essay

Write a reaction essay based on your revised outline from Activity 6. Be sure to refer to *Steps in the Writing Process* in the *Writer's Handbook*.

ACTIVITY 8 | Peer editing your essay

Exchange papers from Activity 7 with a partner. Read your partner's essay. Then use Peer Editing Form 6 in the *Writer's Handbook* to help you comment on your partner's essay. Be sure to offer positive suggestions to help your partner improve his or her writing. Consider your partner's comments as you revise your essay.

ELEMENTS OF GREAT WRITING

Understanding Short-Answer Questions

When students take a test, they are often asked to answer **short-answer questions**. These are also called **essay questions** (although they are often not as long as an essay). Here are some examples of short-answer questions from different academic courses:

COURSE	SHORT-ANSWER EXAM QUESTION
Psychology	Define the following mental disorders: depression, anxiety, and dementia.
History	Classify the major Pacific battles of World War II in terms of the number of soldiers killed on both sides.
Literature	List what you consider to be O. Henry's three best short stories. As you rank them, justify your ranking using the key components of literature (theme, plot, setting, character) presented in this course.
Biology	Explain how blood circulates through your body starting with the heart. List all of the key areas of the heart that are involved in circulation.
Economics	Discuss the recent world economic recession. Include a description of what happened and evaluate the world's major economic powers' responses to the financial crisis.
Engineering	Evaluate Leonardo da Vinci's 15th-century model of the helicopter and compare it to today's helicopter.

Verbs Frequently Used in Short-Answer Questions

Following is a list of common verbs used in short-answer questions:

1. **Define**

   Definitions call for meanings of a concept. One common definition type is the **three-point definition**. The three-point definition begins by explaining what general group the subject is part of. Part two of the definition is an explanation of the parts or special characteristics of the object. The three-part definition ends with an example of the object.

   Exam Question: Define "war."

   Sample Answer:

   War is a conflict between groups of people. War includes soldiers, weapons, and attack and defense strategies. An example of a war is World War II (1939–1945).

2. **Enumerate/List/Recount**

   These verbs ask for the writer to produce a list of items that answer the question. The answer may be introduced by a sentence that is followed by a numbered or bulleted list. Enumerations or lists do not need to be complete sentences.

   Exam Question: List Leonardo da Vinci's most famous ideas and/or inventions.

   Sample Answer:

   The following is a list of Leonardo da Vinci's most famous ideas and/or inventions:
   1. The anemometer, which was used for measuring the speed of wind
   2. The flying machine, a precursor to today's airplane
   3. The helicopter, a machine that was modeled to fly vertically

3. **Categorize/Classify**

   For this type of question, you must put things into groups or categories according to shared qualities or characteristics. Your answer should include an example of the group or category.

   Exam Question: Classify the different kinds of hurricanes.

   Sample Answer:

   Hurricanes are categorized by the speed of wind. According to NASA, there are five categories of hurricanes from 1 to 5, with 5 being the most powerful. A category 5 hurricane has winds of more than 252 km/hr (157 mph). An example of this type of hurricane is Irma, which hit in 2017.

4. Summarize

When an exam question asks for a summary, you should give only the main points or facts. All details, examples, and especially personal observations should not be included.

Exam Question: Summarize the article "Environmental Dangers of the Twenty-First Century" in one paragraph.

Sample Thesis:

The article presents the three main challenges facing the environment today.

5. Explain/Illustrate/Describe/Discuss

A test question with these verbs asks for clarification of a concept. Very often you may use a diagram, graph, or concrete example to explain or illustrate your answer.

Exam Question: Illustrate the process a wind turbine uses to harness energy.

Sample Thesis:

The process of a wind turbine is simple. The wind turns the blades around a rotor. The rotor is connected to a shaft which spins a generator to create electricity.

6. Relate/Compare/Contrast/Distinguish/Differentiate

Test questions with these verbs ask you to explain the relationship of something to something else. You need to explain the connections and associations of these two things, whether they are similar or different.

Exam Question: Relate the large numbers of immigrants to the United States in the early 1900s to the beginning of the Industrial Revolution.

Sample Thesis:

The Industrial Revolution in the U.S. was made possible by the millions of newly arrived immigrants in the early 1900s.

7. Evaluate/Assess/Criticize/Justify/Argue

For this type of question, you are asked to not only understand but also evaluate or judge. This is one of the more difficult short-answer questions to answer because you must use persuasive language in your writing.

Exam Question: Evaluate the performance of the latest tablet computer in terms of memory and speed.

Sample Thesis:

The latest tablet computer may be faster than the previous one, but it has less memory.

ACTIVITY 9 | Asking and answering short-answer questions

Choose three verbs from the box. Write three short-answer questions about different types of academic essays (the focus of this textbook), or on the subject of any of the essays in this book. Underline the verb in each question.

define	evaluate	explain	illustrate	list	summarize

Short-Answer Question: List the three main kinds of shopping options available to consumers.

Short-Answer Response:

1. In-person shopping, which is ideal for shoppers who want to see and touch items before buying them
2. Online shopping, for customers who want to compare availability, price, and quality without leaving home
3. Third-party shopping, for shoppers who have more money than time

(Your questions)

Q1: _____

_____

Q2: _____

_____

Q3: _____

_____

Now exchange textbooks with a classmate. Choose one of your classmate's questions and answer it below. Be sure you understand the verb that is used in the question before writing your answer.

_____

_____

_____

_____

WRITER'S NOTE Using the Space Provided

When you are answering a short-answer question on a test, use the amount of blank (white) space on the test paper as a guide to how much information to write. Your instructors are most likely giving you a hint as to how much to include in your answer. Try to use only the allotted space and avoid writing in the margins and on the back of your exam paper.

Grammar: Adjective Clause Reductions

In Unit 3, you studied adjective clauses. Sometimes an adjective clause can be reduced or shortened to a phrase. To do this, you usually delete the relative pronoun and change the verb. Here are two rules about adjective clause reductions.

1. If the adjective clause contains the verb *be* (in any form), you can omit the relative pronoun and the verb *be*.

   The man **who is *next to me*** must be a diplomat of some kind. → The man next to me must be a diplomat of some kind.

   People **who were *born before 1960 in the United States*** are called 'Baby Boomers.' → People born before 1960 in the United States are called 'Baby Boomers.'

   Hamlet, **which is *one of Shakespeare's most famous plays***, tells the story of Prince Hamlet's revenge for the murder of his father. → *Hamlet,* one of Shakespeare's most famous plays, tells the story of Prince Hamlet's revenge for the murder of his father.

   (This particular reduction is called an *appositive*. It is a noun phrase that comes directly after a noun and defines or explains that word.)

2. You can sometimes reduce adjective clauses without the verb *be*. In this case, omit the relative pronoun and change the verb to *-ing*, or the present participle form.

   We study in a university **which consists of *six separate colleges*.** → We study in a university **consisting of six separate colleges**.

   People **who live *in cities*** generally do not exercise as often as those **who live in rural areas.** → People **living in cities** generally do not exercise as often as those **living in rural areas**.

Actors in London in 2014 perform a scene from William Shakespeare's *Hamlet* to celebrate the 450th anniversary of the author's birth.

ACTIVITY 10 | Reducing adjective clauses

Underline the adjective clause in the following sentences. Write a reduction above the clause.

1. One of the most well-known athletes with a disability is Trischa Zorn, who is a swimmer from the United States.

2. It may not be long until all athletes who are interested in competing in the traditional Olympics can do so.

3. In the end, I am inspired to learn about such courageous individuals who just want to compete.

4. The other tall building in the background is the well-known Chrysler Building, which is another New York landmark.

5. The structure that supports the workers still stands.

6. I specifically admire this human-made tower, which is reaching toward the sky and toward the future.

7. The photo portrays a man who is focused on his job.

8. It is a decades-old photo that reminds us of how much we have accomplished in such a short period of time.

BUILDING BETTER VOCABULARY

WORDS TO KNOW

accomplish (v)	courageous (adj)	reminder (n)
admiration (n)	device (n) AW	represent (v)
advance (n)	impressed (adj)	safety (n)
alter (v) AW	outcome (n) AW	specifically (adv) AW
comfortably (adv)	passionate (adj)	structure (n) AW
competently (adv)	perseverance (n)	visible (adj) AW
construction (n) AW	portray (v) AW	

ACTIVITY 11 | Word associations

Circle the word or phrase that is more closely related to the bold word on the left.

1. admiration	negative feelings	positive feelings
2. advance	forward movement	backward movement
3. competently	done slowly	done well
4. courageous	fearful	not fearful
5. device	intense feeling	physical object
6. outcome	after	before
7. passionate	intense	indifferent
8. portray	assume	represent
9. specifically	detailed	general
10. visible	ears	eyes

ACTIVITY 12 | Collocations

Fill in the blank with the word that most naturally completes the phrase.

admiration	comfortably	reminder	specifically	structure

1. sitting _____

2. mutual _____

3. a helpful _____

4. _____ concerned with

5. a solid _____

construction	courageous	device	outcome	visible

6. a/an _____ attempt

7. a satisfactory _____

8. clearly _____

9. a complex _____

10. under _____

ACTIVITY 13 | Word forms

Complete each sentence with the correct word form. Use the correct form of the verbs.

NOUN	VERB	ADJECTIVE	ADVERB	SENTENCES
accomplishment	accomplish	accomplished		**1.** Gabriel García Márquez is one of Colombia's most _____ writers. **2.** Graduating at the top of his class was his greatest _____.
impression	impress	impressed/ impressive	impressively	**3.** She answered the question from the audience member _____. **4.** Workers who stay late at work and show interest in the business often want to _____ their bosses.
passion		passionate	passionately	**5.** His _____ for football is unbelievable. **6.** Our literature instructor is _____ about 18th-century poetry.
perseverance	persevere			**7.** She _____ in spite of many challenges. **8.** _____ is essential for professional athletes.
safety		safe	safely	**9.** The swimmer was able to _____ cross the English Channel. **10.** It is not difficult to stay _____ during a hurricane if one is prepared.

ACTIVITY 14 | Vocabulary in writing

Choose seven words from Words to Know. Write a complete sentence with each word.

1. _____

2. _____

3. _____

4. _____

5. _____

6. _____

7. _____

The shortest distance to cross the English Channel is 21 miles (33.8 km). The fastest unassisted swim was completed in 6 hours and 55 minutes by Australian Trent Grimsey in 2012.

BUILDING BETTER SENTENCES

ACTIVITY 15 | Correcting word forms

Look at the underlined words. If there is a word form error, write the correction above the word. If the sentence is correct, write *C* next to it.

1. *families*
   More than 42 million <u>family</u> in the United States face the daily challenges of taking care of their <u>elders</u>.

2. It is <u>impossible</u> to quantify how many workers are <u>unhappily</u> at their jobs.

3. Not many students are <u>interesting</u> in joining service clubs because they are too <u>busy</u> with their <u>academically</u> studies.

4. There are actually very few <u>similar</u> between football and rugby.

5. What is the <u>mean</u> of *perpendicul*ar? I am not <u>surely</u>.

6. With two weeks' <u>vacation</u> instead of one, his family has decided to <u>visit</u> the Grand Canyon.

ACTIVITY 16 | Combining sentences

Combine the ideas into one sentence. You may change the word forms, but do not change or omit any ideas. There may be more than one answer.

1. Mount Kilimanjaro is located in Tanzania.
   Mount Kilimanjaro is the tallest mountain.
   The mountain is in Africa.

   _____

   _____

2. Baby giraffes can stand up on their own.
   This happens five hours after they are born.
   Baby giraffes can run.
   This happens 10 hours after they are born.

   _____

   _____

3. "Animal rain" is a phenomenon.
   The phenomenon is fascinating.
   Small animals get sucked up by waterspouts.
   Then they fall to the ground.
   They fall with raindrops.

ACTIVITY 17 | Writing about a photo

On a separate piece of paper, write five to eight sentences about the photo. Try to use at least one adjective clause reduction in your writing.

Skater Lisa van der Geest celebrates a victory in the Netherlands.

TEST PREP

You should spend about 20 minutes on this task (10 minutes per question). Answer the following questions:

Question 1: Summarize the main points of this textbook. (Write at least 100 words.)

Question 2: Evaluate your own academic writing skills. (Write at least 150 words.)

Review each question carefully. Be sure you understand the verbs before answering the writing prompts.

> **TIP**
>
> Follow the guidelines. If the assignment asks for a 150-word response, be sure that your writing response comes close to that. Writers do NOT get extra points for writing more than what is required, and may lose points for writing significantly less.

WRITER'S HANDBOOK

UNDERSTANDING THE WRITING PROCESS

As you learned in Unit 1, writing is a process. Writers rarely write an essay from introduction to conclusion in one sitting. Instead, they follow certain steps. Use these steps as a guideline when you write.

Step 1:   Choose a Topic

Step 2:   Brainstorm

Step 3:   Outline

Step 4:   Write the First Draft

Step 5:   Get Feedback from a Peer

Step 6:   Reread, Rethink, Rewrite

Step 7:   Proofread the Final Draft

Steps in the Writing Process

Step 1: Choose a Topic

Sometimes you will be asked to write an essay on a broad topic such as *An Influential Person*. In this case, you can choose any person you want as long as you can clearly show how that person has influenced you or others. You should try to choose a topic that you are interested in.

For this assignment, imagine that the topic was given: "Write an essay in which you discuss one aspect of being a vegetarian." As you consider the assignment, think about what kind of essay you want to write:

- A classification of the types of vegetarian diets
- A historical account of vegetarianism
- An argument that being a vegetarian is better than eating meat

The type of essay you write (argument, comparison, etc.) will depend on the topic you choose (or are given), and the ideas you decide to develop.

Step 2: Brainstorm

Write every idea about your topic that comes to mind. Some of these ideas will be better than others; write them all. The main purpose of brainstorming is to write as many ideas as possible. If one idea looks promising, circle it or put a check next to it. If you write an idea that you know right away you are not going to use, cross it out.

Brainstorming methods include making lists, clustering similar ideas, or diagramming. Here is an example of a student's brainstorming diagram on the topic of "being a vegetarian."

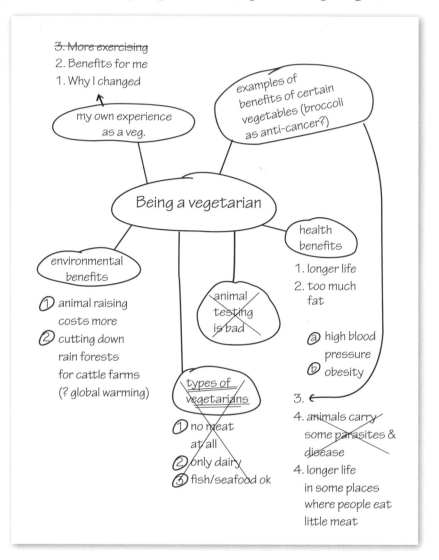

As you can see, the student considered many aspects of being a vegetarian. As she organized her ideas, she wrote "examples of benefits of certain vegetables" as one piece of supporting information. Then she realized that this point would be good in the list of health benefits, so she drew an arrow to show that she should move it there. Since one of her brainstorming ideas (types of vegetarians) lacked supporting details and was not related to her other notes, she crossed it out.

How can you get information for this brainstorming exercise?
- You might search online for an article about vegetarianism.
- You could write a short questionnaire to give to classmates asking them about their personal knowledge of vegetarian practices.
- You could interview an expert on the topic, such as a nutritionist.

Note that any information you get from an outside source needs to be credited in your essay. As you get information, keep notes on your sources. See "Citing Sources and Avoiding Plagiarism" in this *Writer's Handbook* for more information on citing outside sources and referencing.

Step 3: Outline

Next, you should write an outline for your essay. Here is an outline based on the brainstorming notes.

I. Introduction
   A. Hook
   B. Connecting information
   C. Thesis statement

II. Environmental benefits
   A. Rainforests
   B. Global warming

III. Health benefits
   A. Too much fat from meat → obesity → diseases → cancer
   B. High blood pressure and heart disease
   C. Cancer-fighting properties of broccoli and cauliflower, etc.

IV. Counterargument and Refutation
   A. Counterargument: Man is carnivore
   B. Refutation

V. Conclusion
   A. Restate thesis
   B. Opinion

Supporting Details

After you have chosen the main points for your essay, you need to develop some supporting details. You should include examples, reasons, explanations, definitions, or personal experiences.

One common technique for generating supporting details is to ask information questions about the topic: *Who? What? When? Where? Why? How?*

SUPPORT

What benefits does eating vegetables have?

How much longer do vegetarians live?

Why is eating meat a problem?

Step 4: Write the First Draft

In this step, you use information from your brainstorming and outline to draft the essay.

When you write your first draft, pay attention to the language you use. Use a variety of sentence types. Consider your choice of vocabulary. Include specific terminology when possible, and avoid using informal or conversational language.

This first draft may contain errors, such as misspellings, incomplete ideas, and punctuation errors. At this point, you should not worry about correcting the errors. The focus should be on putting your ideas into sentences.

As you write the first draft, you may want to add information or take some out. In some cases, your first draft may not follow your outline exactly. That is OK. Writers do not always stick with their original plan or follow the steps in the writing process in order. Sometimes they go back and forth between steps. The writing process is much more like a cycle than a line.

Step 5: Get Feedback from a Peer

Peer editing is important in the writing process. You do not always see your own mistakes or places where information is missing because you are too close to the paragraph or essay that you wrote. Ask someone to read your draft and give you feedback about your writing. Choose someone that you trust and feel comfortable with. While some people feel uneasy about peer editing, the result is almost always a better essay. You can use the Peer Editing Forms in this *Writer's Handbook* as tools to help your peer editors. Your teacher may also give you feedback on your first draft. As you revise, consider all comments carefully.

Step 6: Reread, Rethink, Rewrite

This step consists of three parts:
1. Reread your essay and any comments from your peers or teacher.
2. Rethink your writing and address the comments.
3. Rewrite the essay.

Step 7: Proofread the Final Draft

Proofreading is the final step. It means reading for grammar, punctuation, and spelling errors and to see if the sentences flow smoothly. One good way to proofread your paper is to set it aside for several hours or a day or two. The next time you read it, your head will be clearer and you will be more likely to see any problems.

On the next two pages is a first draft of the essay on being a vegetarian. It includes comments from the teacher.

Reasons to Be a Vegetarian

1   Do you like burgers? Eating meat, especially beef, is an interesting part
of daily life around the world. <u>In addition,</u> this <u>high eating</u> of meat is a
wrong transition?   *word choice*
major contributing <u>thing</u> that <u>makes</u> many deaths, including deaths from
word choice   word choice
heart-related problems. Vegetarianism has caught on slowly in some parts
transition?
of the world.^Vegetarianism is a way of life that can help improve not only
the quality of lives but also people's longevity.

Be sure your thesis matches your main points. Body par 1 seems to be about environmental impact. Also, you start with burgers but never mention them again. Check your word choice and use of parallel structure.

2   Because demand for meat is so high, cattle are being raised in areas
where the rainforest once stood. [As rain forest land is cleared in order
frag
to make room for the cattle ranches]. The environmental balance is being
upset. This could have serious consequences for us in both the near and
long term. How much of the current global warming is due to man's
disturbing the rain forest?

You need a topic sentence with your first supporting idea: the first reason to be a vegetarian. And add a concluding sentence that restates your main idea.

3   Meat contains a high amount of fat. Eating this fat has been connected
in research with certain kinds of cancer. Furthermore, eating animal
fat can lead to obesity, and obesity can cause different kinds of disease.
what does 'this' refer to?
<u>This</u> results in high blood pressure. Meat is high in cholesterol, and this
adds to the health problems. With the high consumption of animal fat, it
is no wonder that heart disease is a leading killer.

Try a more specific topic sentence relating to health and your thesis.

4   On the other hand, eating a vegetarian diet can improve a person's

health. And vegetables taste good. [*necessary?*] In fact, it can even save lives. Eating

certain kinds of vegetables such as broccoli, brussel sprouts, and cauliflower,

have been [*SVA*] shown to reduce the chance of colon cancer. Vegetables do not

contain the "bad" fats that meat does. Vegetables do not contain cholesterol

either. People with vegetarian diets live longer lives.

5   Although numerous studies have shown the benefits of vegetarianism

for people in general, I know how my life has improved since I decided to

give up meat. In 2010 I saw a show that discussed the problems connected

to animals raised for food. After I saw this show, I decided to try life without

meat. Although it was difficult at first, I have never regretted my decision.

I feel better than before and people tell me I look good. Being a vegetarian

has many benefits. Try it.

*This is a good first draft. I can see that you thought about your topic as you
give some interesting reasons for being a vegetarian. Work on your thesis, topic
sentences, and conclusion. Add a counterargument and a refutation. Consider making
a recommendation in your conclusion.*

*Look for places
to combine short
sentences.
Remember that
you need a
counterargument
and a refutation in an
argument essay. Add
these after your main
arguments and before
your conclusion.*

Now read the final essay this student turned in to her teacher.

Reasons to Be a Vegetarian

1   Eating meat, especially beef, is an integral part of many cultures. Studies show, however, that the consumption of large quantities of meat is a major contributing factor toward a great many deaths, including the unnecessarily high number of deaths from heart-related problems. Although it is not widely adopted in many countries, vegetarianism is a way of life that can have a positive impact on the environment and people's health.

2   Surprising as it may sound, vegetarianism can have beneficial effects on the environment. Because demand for meat animals is so high, cattle are being raised in areas where rain forests once stood. Rain forests have been cleared to make room for cattle ranches, upsetting the environmental balance. One important impact of this kind of deforestation is increased temperatures, which contribute to global warming. If people consumed less meat, the need to clear land for cattle would decrease, helping to restore the ecological balance.

3   More important at an individual level is the question of how eating meat affects a person's health. Meat, unlike vegetables, can contain large amounts of fat. Eating this fat has been connected—in some studies —to certain kinds of cancer. If people cut down on the amount of meat they ate, they would automatically be lowering their risk of disease. Furthermore, eating animal fat can lead to obesity, which can cause numerous health problems. For example, obesity can cause people to become physically inactive and their hearts have to work harder. This results in high blood pressure. Meat is also high in cholesterol, and this only adds to health problems. Eliminating meat from their diet and eating vegetarian food would help people reduce their risk of certain diseases.

4   If people followed vegetarian diets, they would not only be healthier, but also live longer. Eating certain kinds of vegetables, such as broccoli, brussels sprouts, and cauliflower, has been shown to reduce the chance of contracting colon cancer later in life. Vegetables do not contain the "bad" fats that meat does. Vegetables do not contain cholesterol, either. Furthermore, native inhabitants of areas of the world where people eat more vegetables than meat, notably certain areas of Central Asia, routinely live to be over one hundred.

5   Some people argue that, human nature being what it is, it is unhealthy for humans to not eat meat. These same individuals say that humans are naturally carnivores and cannot help wanting to consume a juicy piece of red meat. However, anthropologists have shown that early humans ate meat only when other foods were not abundant. Man is inherently an herbivore, not a carnivore.

6   Numerous scientific studies have shown the benefits of vegetarianism for people in general. There is a common thread for those people who switch from eating meat to consuming only vegetable products. Although the change of diet is difficult at first, most people never regret their decision to become a vegetarian. As more and more people are becoming aware of the risks associated with meat consumption, they too will make the change.

PUNCTUATION

Commas

The comma has different functions. Here are some of the most common:

1. **A comma separates a list of three or more things.**
   She speaks French, English, and Chinese.
   He speaks French and English. (No comma is needed because there are only two items.)

2. **A comma separates two sentences connected by a coordinating conjunction (a combining word) such as *and, but, or, so, for, nor,* and *yet*.**
   Six people took the course, but only five of them passed the test.
   Students can register for classes in person, or they can register by email.

3. **A comma is used to separate an introductory word or phrase from the rest of the sentence.**
   In conclusion, doctors are advising people to take more vitamins.
   Because of the heavy rains, many of the roads were flooded.

4. **A comma is used to separate an appositive from the rest of the sentence. An appositive is a word or group of words that renames a noun.**

   | subject (noun) | appositive | verb |

   Washington, the first president of the United States, was a clever military leader.

5. **A comma is sometimes used with non-restrictive or unnecessary adjective clauses. We use a comma when the information in the clause is unnecessary or extra.**

   The History of Korea, <u>which is on the teacher's desk</u>, is the main book for this class.

   (The name of the book is given, so the information in the adjective clause is not necessary to help the reader identify the book.)

   The book <u>that is on the teacher's desk</u> is the main book for this class.

   (The information in the adjective clause is necessary to identify which book. In this case, do not set off the adjective clause with a comma.)

Apostrophes

Apostrophes have two basic uses in English. They indicate either a contraction or a possession. Note that contractions are seldom used in academic writing.

Contractions: Use an apostrophe in a contraction in place of the letter or letters that have been deleted.

> he's (he is *or* he has), they're (they are), I've (I have), we'd (we would *or* we had)

Possession: Add an apostrophe and the letter *s* after the word. If a plural word already ends in *s*, then just add an apostrophe.

> yesterday's paper
> the boy's books (One boy has some books.)
> the boys' books (Several boys have one or more books.)

Quotation Marks

Here are three of the most common uses for quotation marks.

1. **To mark the exact words that were spoken by someone:**
   The king said, "I refuse to give up my throne." (The period is inside the quotation marks.)
   "None of the solutions is correct," said the professor. (The comma is inside the quotation marks.)

2. **To mark language that a writer has borrowed from another source:**
   The dictionary defines gossip as a "trivial rumor of a personal nature," but I would add that it is usually malicious.
   This research concludes that there was "no real reason to expect this computer software program to produce good results."

3. **To indicate when a word or phrase is being used in a special way:**
   The king believed himself to be the leader of a democracy, so he allowed the prisoner to choose his method of dying. According to the king, allowing this kind of "democracy" showed that he was indeed a good ruler.

Semicolons

The function of a semicolon is similar to that of a period. However, a semicolon suggests a stronger relationship between the sentences.

> Joey loves to play tennis. He has been playing since he was ten years old.

> Joey loves to play tennis; he has been playing since he was ten years old.

Both sentence pairs are correct. Notice that *he* is not capitalized in the second example.

A semicolon is often used with transition words like *however*, *therefore*, and *in addition*.

> The price of gas is increasing; **therefore**, more people are taking public transportation.

SENTENCE TYPES

English has three types of sentences: simple, compound, and complex. These labels indicate how the information in a sentence is organized, not how difficult the content is.

Simple Sentences

Simple sentences usually contain one subject and one verb.

>   S   V
> **Children** <u>love</u> electronic devices.

>   V   S   V
> <u>Does</u> **this** <u>sound</u> like a normal routine?

Sometimes simple sentences can contain more than one subject or verb.

>   S   S   V
> **Brazil** and **the United States** <u>are</u> large countries.

>   S   V   V
> <u>Brazil</u> **is** in South America and **has** a large population.

Compound Sentences

Compound sentences are usually made up of two simple sentences (independent clauses). The two sentences are connected with a coordinating conjunction such as *and, but, or, yet, so,* and *for.* A comma is used before the coordinating conjunction.

> Megan studied hard**, but** she did not pass the final test.

Complex Sentences

Complex sentences contain one independent clause and at least one dependent clause. In most complex sentences, the dependent clause is an adverb clause. (Other complex sentences have dependent adjective clauses or dependent noun clauses.) Adverb clauses begin with subordinating conjunctions, such as *while, although, because,* and *if.*

In the examples below, the adverb clauses are underlined, and the subordinating conjunctions are boldfaced. Notice that the subordinating conjunctions are part of the dependent clauses.

> independent clause   dependent clause
> The hurricane struck **while** <u>we were at the mall</u>.

> dependent clause   independent clause
> **After** <u>the president gave his speech</u>, he answered the reporters' questions.

Dependent clauses must be attached to an independent clause. They cannot stand alone as a sentence. If they are not attached to another sentence, they are called fragments, or incomplete sentences. Look at these examples:

Fragment: After the president gave his speech.
Complete Sentence: After the president gave his speech, he answered the questions.

CONNECTORS

Using connectors will help your ideas flow. Three types of connectors are coordinating conjunctions, subordinating conjunctions, and transitions.

Coordinating Conjunctions

Coordinating conjunctions join two independent clauses to form a compound sentence. Use a comma before a coordinating conjunction in a compound sentence.

Independent clause, +   coordinating +   independent clause.
                            conjunction

The exam was extremely difficult, **but** all of the students received a passing score.

Subordinating Conjunctions

Subordinating conjunctions introduce a dependent clause in a complex sentence.

When a dependent clause begins a sentence, use a comma to separate it from the independent clause.

Dependent clause,   +   independent clause.

Although the exam was extremely difficult, all of the students received a passing score.

Subordinating conjunction

When a dependent clause comes after an independent clause, no comma is used.

Independent clause   +   dependent clause.

All of the students received a passing score **although** the exam was extremely difficult.

subordinating conjunction

Transition Words

Transition words show the relationship between ideas in sentences. A transition followed by a comma can begin a sentence.

Independent clause.   Transition,   independent clause.

The exam was extremely difficult. **However,** all of the students received a passing score.

A transition word followed by a comma can also come after a semicolon. Notice that in the independent clause that follows the semicolon, the first word is not capitalized.

Independent clause.   Transition,   independent clause.

The exam was extremely difficult; **however,** all of the students received a passing score.

USEFUL WORDS AND PHRASES

COMPARING	
Comparative adjective	New York is **larger than** Rhode Island.
Comparative adverb	A jet flies **faster than** a helicopter.
In comparison, …	Canada has provinces. **In comparison,** Brazil has states.
Compared to … Similar to … Like …	**Compared to** these roses, those roses last a long time.
Both … and	**Both** models **and** real planes have similar controls.
Likewise, … Similarly, …	Students spend hours each day developing their language skills to enhance their writing. **Likewise,** ballerinas spend countless hours in the gym each week increasing their accuracy and endurance.

CONTRASTING	
In contrast, …	Algeria is a very large country. **In contrast,** the U.A.E. is very small.
Contrasted with In contrast to	**In contrast to** Chicago, Miami has only two seasons: a very mild winter and a very long summer.
Although Even though Though	**Though** London in 1900 was quite different from London in 2000 in many ways, important similarities existed in population, technology, and transportation.
Unlike …	**Unlike** Chicago, the problem in Miami is not the cold but rather the heat.
However,	Canada has provinces. **However,** Brazil has states.
On the one hand, On the other hand,	**On the one hand,** Maggie loved to travel. **On the other hand,** she hated to be away from her home.

SHOWING CAUSE AND EFFECT	
Because Since	**Because** their races are longer, distance runners need to be mentally strong.
cause lead to result in	An earthquake can **cause** tidal waves and *can cause* massive destruction.
As a result of, Because of,	**Because of** the economic sanctions, the unemployment rate rose.
Therefore, As a result,	Markets fell. **Therefore,** millions of people lost their life savings.

STATING AN OPINION	
I believe / think / feel / agree / that	**I believe that** using electronic devices on a plane should be allowed.
In my opinion / view / experience,	**In my opinion,** talking on a cell phone in a movie theater is extremely rude.
For this reason,	**For this reason,** voters should not pass this law.
There are many benefits / advantages / disadvantages	**There are many benefits** to swimming every day.

ARGUING	
It is important to remember	**It is important to remember** that school uniforms would only be worn during school hours.
According to a recent survey,	**According to a recent survey,** the biggest fear of most people is public speaking.
For these reasons,	**For these reasons,** public schools should require uniforms.
Without a doubt,	**Without a doubt,** students ought to learn a foreign language.

GIVING A COUNTERARGUMENT	
Proponents / Opponents may say	**Opponents** of uniforms **say** that students who wear uniforms cannot express their individuality.
One could argue that, but	**One could argue that** working for a small company is very exciting, **but** it can also be more stressful than a job in a large company.
Some people believe that	**Some people believe that** nuclear energy is the way of the future.
Although it is true that…	**Although it is true that** taking online classes can be convenient, it is difficult for many students to stay on task.

CITING SOURCES AND AVOIDING PLAGIARISM

When writing a paragraph or an essay, you should use you own words for the most part. Sometimes, however, you may want to use ideas that you have read in a book, in an article, on a website, or even heard in a speech. It can make the paragraph or essay more interesting, more factual, or more relevant to the reader. For example, if you are writing a paragraph about a recent election, you may want to use a quotation from a politician. In this case, you must indicate that the words are not your own, but that they come from someone else. Indicating that your words are not original is called **citing**. In academic writing, it is necessary to cite all sources of information that are not original.

If the information does not come from your head, it must be cited. If you do not—whether intentionally or unintentionally—give credit to the original author, you are **plagiarizing**, or stealing, someone else's words. This is academic theft, and most institutions take this very seriously.

To avoid plagiarism, it is important to use quotes or a paraphrase which includes an in-text citation, and add a reference or bibliography at the end of your writing.

Using Quotes

Quotations are used when you want to keep the source's exact words. Here are some verbs that are often used to introduce quotes.

argue	describe	insist	predict	say
claim	find	point out	report	state

Here are three different examples of quoting a sentence from a text.

Original*: There is absolutely no empirical evidence—quantitative or qualitative —to support the familiar notion that monolingual dictionaries are better than bilingual dictionaries for understanding and learning L2.

Quote 1: According to Folse (2004), "There is absolutely no empirical evidence—quantitative or qualitative—to support the familiar notion that monolingual dictionaries are better than bilingual dictionaries for understanding and learning L2."

Quote 2: And while instructors continue to push for monolingual dictionaries, "there is absolutely no empirical evidence—quantitative or qualitative—to support the familiar notion that monolingual dictionaries are better than bilingual dictionaries for understanding and learning L2" (Folse, 2004).

Quote 3: As Folse points out, "There is absolutely no empirical evidence – quantitative or qualitative—to support the familiar notion that monolingual dictionaries are better than bilingual dictionaries for understanding and learning L2" (2004).

Note that brief in-text citations in the body of your work are appropriate for quotes like these. But you must also list the complete source at the end of your work.

*Folse, Keith. *Vocabulary Myths: Applying Second Language Research to Classroom Teaching*. University of Michigan Press, 2004.

Paraphrasing

Sometimes you may want to paraphrase or summarize outside information. In this case, the same rules still hold true. If the ideas are not yours, they must be cited.

Original*:	Every year, the town of Vinci, Italy, receives as many as 500,000 visitors—people coming in search of its most famous son, Leonardo.
Paraphrase:	Although a small town, Vinci is visited by many tourists because it is the birthplace of Leonardo da Vinci (Herrick, 2009).
Original*:	This quiet, unimposing hill town is relatively unchanged from the time of Leonardo.
Paraphrase:	Herrick (2009) explains that even after 500 years, the town of Vinci has remained pretty much the same.

*Herrick, Troy. *"Vinci: A Visit to Leonardo's Home Town."* Offbeat Travel, Updated January 5, 2016, www.offbeattravel.com/vinci-italy-davinci-home.html.

Bibliography

At the end of your paragraph or essay, you must list the sources you used. There are many types of citation styles. Among the most commonly used are APA (American Psychological Association), Chicago, and MLA (Modern Language Association), with MLA being the most common in the liberal arts and humanities fields. Ask your instructor which one you should use. The References (APA) or Works Cited page (MLA) at the end of your work should include complete sources for all quotes and paraphrases, but also any source that helped you develop your work. Here are some guidelines for referencing different works using MLA:

SOURCE	INFORMATION TO INCLUDE	EXAMPLE
Book	Last name of author, First name. *Title of Book.* Publisher, year of publication.	Folse, Keith. *Vocabulary Myths: Applying Second Language Research to Classroom Teaching.* University of Michigan Press, 2004.
Online Article	Last name of author, First name (if there is one). "*Title of Web Page.*" Title of Website, Publisher, Date published, URL.	"*Becoming a Vegetarian.*" Harvard Health Publishing, Harvard University, October 2009, updated December 4, 2017, www.health.harvard.edu/staying-healthy/becoming-a-vegetarian (Note that you should remove http:// and https:// from the URL.)
Website	Last name of author, First name (if there is one). "*Title of Web Page.*" Title of Website, Publisher, Date published (if given), URL.	"*The Complete Guide to MLA & Citations.*" Citation Machine, a Chegg Service, Study Break Media, www.citationmachine.net/mla/cite-a-website.
Newspaper	Last name of author, First name. "Title of Article." *Name of Newspaper*, Date, page numbers.	Smith, Steven. "What To Do in Case of Emergencies." *USA Today*, December 13, 2008, 2–3.

TEST TAKING TIPS

Before Writing

- Before you begin writing, make sure that you understand the assignment. Underline key words in the writing prompt. Look back at the key words as you write to be sure you are answering the question correctly and staying on topic.
- Take five minutes to plan before you start writing. First, list out all the ideas you have about the topic. Then think about which ideas have the best supporting examples or ideas. Use this information to choose your main idea(s). Circle the supporting information you want to include. Cross out other information.
- Organize your ideas before you write. Review the list you have created. Place a number next to each idea, from most important to least important. In this way, if you do not have enough time to complete your writing, you will be sure that the most relevant information will be included in your essay.

While Writing

For Paragraphs

- Be sure that your topic sentence has a logical controlling idea. Remember that your topic sentence guides your paragraph. If the topic sentence is not clear, the reader will have difficulty following your supporting ideas.
- It is important for your writing to look like a paragraph. Be sure to indent the first sentence. Write the rest of the sentences from margin to margin. Leave an appropriate amount of space after your periods. These small details make your paragraph easier to read and understand.

For Essays

- Be sure that your thesis statement responds to the prompt and expresses your main idea. The thesis may also include your points of development. Remember that if your thesis statement is not clear, the reader will have difficulty following the supporting ideas in the body paragraphs.
- Readers will pay special attention to the last paragraph of your essay, so take two or three minutes to check it before you submit it. Make sure your concluding paragraph restates information in the introduction paragraph and offers a suggestion, gives an opinion, asks a question, or makes a prediction.

For Either Paragraphs or Essays

- Do not write more than is requested. If the assignment asks for a 150-word response, be sure that your writing response comes close to that. Students do not get extra points for writing more than what is required.
- If you are using a word processor, choose a font that is academic and clear like Times New Roman or Calibri. Choose an appropriate point size like 12. Use double space or one and a half space so that it is easier to read. Remember to indent paragraphs and leave a space between sentences.

- Once you pick a side (agree or disagree), include only the ideas that support that side. Sometimes you may have ideas for both sides. If this happens, choose the side that is easier for you to write about. If you do not have an opinion, choose the side you can write about best, even if you do not believe in it. You receive points for your writing skill, not your true personal beliefs.

Word Choice
- Avoid using words such as *always*, *never*, *all*, and *none*. You cannot give enough proof for these words. Instead, use words such as *probably*, *often*, *most*, *many*, *almost never*, and *almost none*.
- Avoid using general or vague vocabulary. Words such as *nice*, *good*, and *very* can often be changed to more specific terms, such as *friendly*, *fabulous*, and *incredibly*. Be more specific in your word choice.
- Avoid conversational or informal language in academic writing.

Development
- Avoid information that is too general. When possible, give specific examples. Good writers want to show that they have thought about the subject and provide interesting and specific information in their writing.

After Writing
- Leave time to proofread your paragraph or essay. Check for subject-verb agreement, correct use of commas and end punctuation, and for clear ideas that all relate to the topic sentence (paragraphs) or thesis statement (essay).
- Check for informal language such as contractions or slang. These do not belong in academic writing.

Managing Time
- It is common to run out of time at the end of a writing test. Once you have written your introduction and the body paragraphs, check your remaining time. Then read through what you have written to check for the clarity of your ideas. If you are running out of time, write a very brief conclusion.

PEER EDITING FORMS

Peer Editing Form for Outlines

Reader: _____ Date: _____

1. What is the topic of the essay? _____

2. Is there an effective hook?   ☐ Yes   ☐ No

3. Is the thesis statement clear?   ☐ Yes   ☐ No

4. What do you expect to read about in this essay? _____

5. How many paragraphs are going to be in the essay? _____

6. Does the topic sentence in each body paragraph relate to the thesis?   ☐ Yes   ☐ No

   If no, explain. _____

7. What kind of ending will the essay have—a suggestion, prediction, question, or opinion?

   _____

8. Do you have any questions about the outline?   ☐ Yes   ☐ No

   If yes, write them here: _____

   _____

Peer Editing Form 1

Reader: _____ Date: _____

1. What is the topic of the essay? _____

2. Does the introduction have an effective hook? ☐ Yes ☐ No

3. Is the thesis statement clear? ☐ Yes ☐ No

   Write it here: _____

   _____

4. Based on the introduction, what do you expect to read about in this essay?

   _____

5. Does each body paragraph have a topic sentence related to the thesis statement?

   ☐ Yes ☐ No

   If no, explain. _____

6. Does the essay include at least two vocabulary words or phrases from the unit? ☐ Yes ☐ No

   List them here: _____

7. Check all that apply: The conclusion

   ☐ summarizes the main points

   ☐ offers a suggestion, makes a prediction, asks a question, or gives an opinion

8. What do you like best about this essay? _____

   _____

9. Is there any place where you want more information? ☐ Yes ☐ No

   If yes, where? _____

Peer Editing Form 2

Reader: _____ Date: _____

1. What is the topic of the cause-effect essay? _____

2. Which method does it follow: focus-on-causes or focus-on-effects? _____

3. Does the introduction have an effective hook?   ☐ Yes   ☐ No

4. Is the thesis statement clear?   ☐ Yes   ☐ No

   Is it direct or indirect? _____

   Write it here: _____

   _____

5. Based on the introduction, what do you expect to read about in this essay?

   _____

6. Does each body paragraph have a topic sentence related to the thesis statement?

   ☐ Yes   ☐ No

   If no, explain. _____

7. Does the essay include connectors that show cause or effect?   ☐ Yes   ☐ No

   List them here: _____

8. Does the essay include at least two vocabulary words or phrases from the unit? ☐ Yes ☐ No

   List them here: _____

9. Check all that apply: The conclusion

   ☐ summarizes the main points

   ☐ offers a suggestion, makes a prediction, asks a question, or gives an opinion

10. What do you like best about this essay? _____

    _____

11. Is there any place where you want more information?   ☐ Yes   ☐ No

    If yes, where? _____

Peer Editing Form 3

Reader: _____   Date: _____

1. What is the topic of the comparison essay? _____

2. Which method does it follow: block or point-by-point? _____

3. Does the introduction have an effective hook?   ☐ Yes   ☐ No

4. Is the thesis statement clear?   ☐ Yes   ☐ No

    Is it direct or indirect? _____

    Write it here: _____

    _____

5. Based on the introduction, what do you expect to read about in this essay?

    _____

6. Does each body paragraph have a topic sentence related to the thesis statement? ☐ Yes ☐ No

    If no, explain. _____

7. Does the essay include connectors that show comparison, contrast, or concession between

    sentences?   ☐ Yes   ☐ No

    List them here: _____

8. Does the essay include at least two vocabulary words or phrases from the unit? ☐ Yes ☐ No

    List them here: _____

9. Check all that apply: The conclusion

    ☐ summarizes the main points

    ☐ offers a suggestion, makes a prediction, asks a question, or gives an opinion

10. What do you like best about this essay? _____

    _____

11. Is there any place where you want more information?   ☐ Yes   ☐ No

    If yes, where? _____

Peer Editing Form 4

Reader: _____ Date: _____

1. What is the topic of the argument essay? _____

2. Does the introduction have an effective hook? _____

3. Is the thesis statement clear and effective?   ☐ Yes   ☐ No

    Write it here: _____

    _____

    Does it have two viewpoints?   ☐ Yes   ☐ No

4. Based on the introduction, what do you expect to read about in this essay?

    _____

5. Does each body paragraph have a topic sentence related to the thesis statement? ☐ Yes   ☐ No

    If no, explain. _____

6. Does the essay include a counterargument and refutation?   ☐ Yes   ☐ No

7. Does the essay include modals to control the tone?   ☐ Yes   ☐ No

    List them here: _____

8. Does the essay include at least two vocabulary words or phrases from the unit? ☐ Yes   ☐ No

    List them here: _____

9. Check all that apply: The conclusion

    ☐ summarizes the main points

    ☐ offers a suggestion, makes a prediction, asks a question, or gives an opinion

10. What do you like best about this essay? _____

    _____

11. Is there any place where you want more information?   ☐ Yes   ☐ No

    If yes, where? _____

Peer Editing Form 5

Reader: _____ Date: _____

1. What is the topic of the problem-solution essay? _____

2. Does the introduction have an effective hook?   ☐ Yes   ☐ No

3. Does the introduction give background information or history about the problem?

                                                                    ☐ Yes   ☐ No

4. Is the thesis statement clear?   ☐ Yes   ☐ No

   Write it here: _____

   _____

5. Based on the introduction, what do you expect to read about in this essay?

   _____

6. Does each body paragraph have a topic sentence related to the thesis statement?

                                                                    ☐ Yes   ☐ No

   If no, explain. _____

7. Does the essay offer one or two solid solutions to the problem? ☐ Yes   ☐ No

   Write the solution(s) here: _____

8. Does the essay include at least five adverb clauses?   ☐ Yes   ☐ No

   List them here: _____

9. Check all that apply: The conclusion

   ☐ summarizes the main points

   ☐ encourages the reader to take action to help correct the problem

10. What do you like best about this essay? _____

    _____

11. Is there any place where you want more information?   ☐ Yes   ☐ No

    If yes, where? _____

Peer Editing Form 6

Reader: _____ Date: _____

1. What is the topic of the reaction essay? _____

2. Does the introduction have an effective hook? ☐ Yes ☐ No

3. Does the introduction provide a summary of the prompt? ☐ Yes ☐ No

4. Is the thesis statement clear? ☐ Yes ☐ No

    Write it here: _____

    _____

5. Based on the introduction, what do you expect to read about in this essay?

    _____

6. Does each body paragraph have a topic sentence that states a reaction? ☐ Yes ☐ No

    If no, explain. _____

7. Does each body paragraph have supporting details? ☐ Yes ☐ No

    If no, explain. _____

8. Check all that apply: The conclusion

    ☐ restates the writer's overall reaction to the prompt

    ☐ states whether the prompt had an effect on the writer

    ☐ offers an opinion about the prompt

9. What do you like best about this essay? _____

    _____

10. Is there any place where you want more information? ☐ Yes ☐ No

    If yes, where? _____

VOCABULARY INDEX

Word	Page	CEFR† Level	Word	Page	CEFR† Level	Word	Page	CEFR† Level
accessible*	107	B2	disruptive	72	C2	irresponsible	40	B2
accomplish	153	C1	distinguish	49	B2	isolation*	103	C1
accumulate*	136	C2	diversity*	72	C1	keep track of	129	C1
admiration	150	B2	drawback	12	C1	lack of	8	B2
advance	150	B2	eliminate*	77	C1	lead to	8	B2
affordable	82	C1	enforce*	135	C1	lenient	80	C2
alter*	150	B2	ethnic*	72	C1	maintain*	40	B2
appreciate*	12	B2	everyday	103	off-list	massive	72	B2
asset	72	C1	exemplify	40	C2	measure	129	B2
associated with	99	B2	exposure*	52	C1	mediate*	24	off-list
assume*	15	B2	familiarize	49	C2	merit	99	C1
authentic	103	C1	fatigued*	43	off-list	monitor*	80	B2
automatically*	129	B2	focus on*	72	B2	motive*	40	B2
availability*	6	B2	fundamental*	24	C2	numerous	82	C1
be concerned about	8	B2	generate*	129	B2	obtain*	6	B2
budget	129	B2	guaranteed*	107	B2	official	135	B2
burden	82	C1	harm	80	B2	on the surface	99	B2
capacity*	107	B2	have a point	49	off-list	opponent	99	B2
collaboration	135	C1	have the means to	15	off-list	outcome*	150	C1
comfortably	153	B2	impact*	52	B2	overall*	8	B2
commitment*	107	B2	implement*	99	B2	overwhelming	77	C1
compelling	49	C1	imply*	43	C2	passionate	150	B2
competently	153	C1	impressed	150	B2	permanently	8	B2
concept*	6	B2	in essence*	80	C2	perseverance	150	C2
consequence*	40	B2	in terms of	12	B2	portray*	153	C2
consideration	77	B2	in the long run	52	off-list	pose*	52	C1
construction*	153	B2	in the meantime	43	B2	pretend	80	B2
core*	72	C2	inadequate*	103	C1	prevalent	8	off-list
correlation*	43	off-list	inappropriate*	49	C1	primarily*	6	B2
countless	22	C1	incident*	99	B2	prominent*	129	C1
courageous	150	C1	income*	107	B2	propose	135	B2
creation*	107	B2	innovation*	107	C1	prosperity	107	C1
crisis	15	B2	integral*	82	C1	punishment*	99	B2
crucial*	22	B2	integrity*	129	C2	purchase*	77	B2
currently	49	B2	intensify*	103	C2	recognition	135	C2
device*	150	B2	intimidate	77	off-list	regardless of	12	C1
disposal*	135	B2	intrigued	52	off-list	regulation*	135	B2
						remark	107	B2

Word	Page	CEFR† Level	Word	Page	CEFR† Level
remarkable	72	B2	thrive	43	C1
reminder	153	C1	trustworthy	129	C1
represent	153	B2	undergo*	49	C1
resource*	135	B2	unique*	72	B2
risk	8	B2	unity*	99	C1
roughly	22	B2	unprecedented*	103	C2
safety	153	B2	usage*	129	C1
scenario*	80	C2	use up	135	B2
selection*	12	B2	visible*	153	B2
somewhat*	40	C1	wealth	99	B2
specifically*	153	C1	when it comes to	80	C1
structure*	153	B2	widespread*	129	C1
substantial	43	B2	worldwide	103	B2
tend to	6	B2			

Every unit in *Great Writing* highlights key academic vocabulary, indicated by **AW**. These words have been selected using the Academic Word List (Coxhead, 2000) and the New Academic Word List (Browne, C., Culligan, B. & Phillips, J., 2013).

*These words are on the AWL or NAWL.

†Vocabulary was also chosen based on levels of The Common European Framework of Reference for Languages (CEFR). CEFR is an international standard for describing language proficiency. *Great Writing 4* is most appropriate for students at CEFR levels B2–C1.

The target vocabulary is at the CEFR levels as shown.

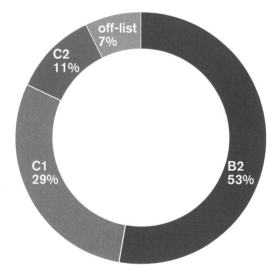

INDEX

A

Academic Words (AW), 32, 58, 83, 116, 138, 164
Academic writing, 36–37, 62–67, 88–95, 120–123, 143–147, 156–159, 169
  sentence variety, 133
  stating main idea, 20
Adjective clause reductions, 163–164
Adjective clauses, 81–82
Adverb clauses, 114, 133–134
Appeal to authority, 112
Argument essays, 96–123
  counterargument, 98, 110
  defined, 4
  faulty logic, 112–113
  outlining, 102–103, 121–122
  planning, 120–121
  refutation of opposing viewpoint, 98, 110
  supporting details, 103
  thesis statement, 105
  topic selection, 98
Asking questions, 76
Audience, 98

B

Block method, 71
Body of essay, 4–5, 27–30, 151–152
Body paragraphs
  in cause-effect essay, 40
  in problem-solution essays, 126
Brainstorming, 36, 62–63, 88–89, 127
Building Better Sentences, 34–35, 60–62, 86–87, 118–119, 140–142, 168–169
Building Better Vocabulary, 32–34, 58–60, 83–85, 116–118, 138–140, 164–167

C

Cause-effect essays, 38–67
  defined, 4, 40
  focus-on-causes method, 40
  focus-on-effects method, 40
  outlining, 46–48, 64–65
  supporting details, 49
  topic selection, 63, 67
Cause-effect words and phrases, 51
Checking the first and last paragraphs, 31
Citing sources, 115
Cluster diagrams, 63
Commas, 79, 81
Common comparisons, 70
Comparison connectors, 79

Comparison essays, 68–95
  defined, 4, 70
  organization, 71
  outlining, 75–76, 92–93
  supporting details, 77
  topic selection, 89
Comparison words and phrases, 79
Complex sentences, 82, 133
Con statements, 98
Concession connectors, 79
Concise phrases, 55–57
Concluding paragraphs, 31, 70, 126
Conclusion
  of essay, 4–5
  of reaction essays, 152
  restating the thesis, 5
  suggestion, predictions, questions, or opinions in, 5, 31
  writing, 31
Connecting information, 20
Connectors and transitions, 51, 79–80, 133
Contrast connectors, 79
Controlling ideas, 5
Counterargument, 98, 110
Crediting outside sources, 45

D

Dependent clauses, 54
Detailed outline, 27, 29
Direct thesis statements, 21
Documenting information sources, 115

E

Editing, 67, 94, 123, 147, 159
Either/or arguments, 113
Essay questions, 159–161
Essays
  argument, 4, 96–123
  cause-effect, 4, 38–67
  comparison, 5, 68–95
  definition and types of, 4
  five-paragraph, 4
  number of paragraphs in, 146
  parts of, 4–5, 8
  persuasive, 4, 96–123
  planning, 120–121
  problem-solution, 4, 124–147
  reaction and response, 148–169
Events related by sequence, 112

F

Facts, focus on, 106
Faulty logic, 112–113
First drafts, 36, 66
Five-paragraph essays, 4
Focus on facts, 106
Focusing your essay, 127

Focus-on-causes method, 40, 46–47
Focus-on-effects method, 40, 48

G

General outline, 27–28
Generalizations, 112
Grammar
  adjective clause reductions, 163–164
  adjective clauses, 81–82
  adverb clauses, 114, 133–134
  cause-effect structures, 51
  connectors, 51, 79–80, 133
  dependent clauses, 54
  modals, 107
  noun clauses, 54
  subject adjective clauses, 81–82
  subordinating conjunctions, 133–134
  transition words, 51
  verbs, 160–161
Great writing, elements of
  in argument essays, 98
  in cause-effect essay, 40
  in comparison essay, 70–71
  parts of essays, 4–5
  in problem-solution essays, 126–127
  in reaction essays, 150–152
  short-answer questions, 159–161

H

Hasty generalizations, 112
Hook, sentence, 8, 19–20

I

Indirect thesis statements, 21
Introduction
  of essay, 4–5, 151
  thesis statement, 5
Introductory paragraphs, 18–21, 126

L

Loaded words, 113

M

Main idea vs. hook, 20
Modals, 107

N

Noun clauses, 54

O

Observations, writing, 153
Opinions, in conclusions, 5, 31
Organization
  methods of, 71
  patterns of, 150
Outlining
  argument and persuasive essays, 102–103, 121–122